REFLECTIONS
OF GOD'S
POETRY BOOKS

JULIE RYAN

WESTBOW
P R E S S®
A DIVISION OF THOMAS NELSON
& ZONDERVAN

WestBow Press books may be ordered through booksellers or by contacting:

WestBow Press
A Division of Thomas Nelson & Zondervan
1663 Liberty Drive
Bloomington, IN 47403
www.westbowpress.com
844-714-3454

Scripture quotations are taken from the Holy Bible, New Living Translation,
copyright © 1996, 2004, 2015 by Tyndale House Foundation. Used by permission
of Tyndale House Publishers Inc., Carol Stream, Illinois 60188. All rights reserved.

ISBN: 979-8-3850-3603-5 (sc)
ISBN: 979-8-3850-3602-8 (e)

Library of Congress Control Number: 2024921656

Print information available on the last page.

WestBow Press rev. date: 11/06/2024

I will study your commandments
and reflect on your ways.
Psalm 119:15

Heavenly Father,
As I reflect on your Word,
help me to understand and apply
your truths to my life.
In Jesus' name I pray,
Amen

CONTENTS

Job

Psalms

Proverbs

Ecclesiastes

Song of Songs

Song of Songs

✧ ✧ ✧

The Book of
Job

JOB 1

Verse 21: He said, "I came naked from my mother's womb, and I will be naked when I leave. The Lord gave me what I had, and the Lord has taken it away. Praise the name of the Lord!"

Reflection:

God allows tests into our lives to reveal to us the strong and weak areas of our faith. God already knows how we will respond, so testing is not for his benefit, it's for ours.

Job was described by God himself as being the finest man in all the earth, but God allowed Satan to test him. We can be walking in the center of God's will, doing everything right, and still be tested. However, nothing can come our way without God's approval. Even Satan must ask God for permission to test us within the boundaries set by God. Job lost all his animals, farm hands, shepherds, servants, sons, and daughters—on the same day. But Job did not sin by blaming God.

Job's response to God is a model of strong faith. We may not always understand our circumstances, but God is always worthy of our worship—even in the midst of suffering.

JOB 2

Verse 10b: "Should we accept only good things from the hand of God and never anything bad?"

Reflection:

Satan's prime targets are people like Job—the finest, blameless people of integrity who fear God and stay away from evil. Satan failed in his first attempt to make Job curse God by killing his animals, employees, and children without cause. So Satan asked God for permission to take away Job's health and struck him with terrible boils from head to toe. But even with this second satanic attack, Job said nothing wrong.

Satan hasn't changed. He wants to destroy all people, but especially the children of God. Since he can't drag us to hell, he tries to destroy our testimony by attacking our health, our family, our job, our reputation—whatever will inflict the most pain and make us turn away from God.

There are things happening in the unseen world that affect our lives—a larger story centered on God, not us. When we don't know why God permits bad things to happen, we must learn to feel comfortable allowing the mystery of our suffering to coexist with our faith in God.

When we, God's beloved children, do not understand what God's hand is doing, may we trust his heart.

JOB 3

Verses 25-26: "What I always feared has happened to me. What I dreaded has come true. I have no peace, no quietness. I have no rest; only trouble comes."

Reflection:

These are the words of Job after a week of sitting in silence with his friends. Job's mind, the devil's target, turned dark, and he cursed the day that he was born.

God knows the emotional trauma of suffering and loss. Just as God did not condemn Job's dark thoughts, sorrow, grief, or questions, he will not condemn us for turning to him with our true feelings and deepest wounds.

It is natural for us to have a season of darkness, especially when Satan attacks us—that's his goal. But the longer we choose to stay in that mindset, the harder it will be for us to get out. So, we must choose to let the Holy Spirit control our mind and refocus on God. We must ask our heavenly Father for help in prayer and trust him to come to our rescue.

JOB 4

Verses 8-9: "My experience shows that those who plant trouble and cultivate evil will harvest the same. A breath from God destroys them. They vanish in a blast of his anger."

Reflection:

Job was an innocent man who feared God and who lived a life of integrity. In the past, when people experienced personal trials, Job was the one who encouraged, strengthened, and supported them. Now that Job was going through troubles of his own, he was terrified and losing heart.

We know that Satan was the one planting trouble in Job's life—and Satan is the one cultivating evil in our world today. But we can have hope because the Bible says that when the Lord Jesus returns, he will slay Satan with the breath of his mouth and destroy him by the splendor of his coming. Even though justice doesn't always happen now, and innocent people sometimes suffer, we can be confident that, in the end, God will deliver justice.

JOB 5

Verses 17-18: "But consider the joy of those corrected by God. Do not despise the discipline of the Almighty when you sin. For though he wounds, he also bandages. He strikes, but his hands also heal."

Reflection:

God disciplines those he loves. So, as children accepted by God through Christ, we can expect his divine discipline in our lives. Our heavenly Father only does what is good for us so that we can share in his holiness. Therefore, even though discipline is not enjoyable, it is a form of training that makes us more like Jesus.

When we submit to God's training, we will learn how to live good, right, and peaceful lives. So don't give up when the Lord corrects you—trust him, patiently endure, and think about God's promise of joy.

JOB 6

Verses 2-3a: "If my misery could be weighed and my troubles be put on the scales, they would outweigh all the sands of the sea."

Reflection:

Sometimes, we feel like Job. Like we don't have the strength to endure. Like we have nothing to live for. Like we are utterly helpless. And maybe, like Job, we wish that God would reach out his hand and kill us.

But despite the pain he endured, Job did not deny God. Despite the accusations of his friends, Job did not reject the words of the Holy One. And despite the assumption of guilt by others, Job knew that he had done nothing wrong.

May we take comfort in knowing that God understands the reason for our circumstances. May we realize that God is with us in our pain, even if we can't feel him. And may we remember that God will give us the grace we need to endure whatever he allows to pass through his nail-scarred hands into our lives.

JOB 7

Verse 1a: "Is not all human life a struggle?"

Reflection:

Job experienced long, weary nights of misery as he tossed and turned in bed until dawn. He had terrifying dreams and visions. His body was covered with maggots, scabs, and oozing sores. And he thought he would never feel happiness again.

Everyone will have seasons of pain, anguish, and suffering. As the days drag on, our soul may grow bitter. We long for comfort, and we hate our lives. We wonder, "What have I done to cause this? Have I sinned? Am I God's target?"

As believers and followers of Jesus, we know that not even the Son of God was excluded from experiencing intense pain and suffering. So when our faith is tested by suffering and we, like Job, would rather die than go on living in pain, we know that we are being transformed into the likeness of Christ through our circumstances.

Does it mean that God no longer loves us when we have trouble or calamity in our lives? No! Did God the Father stop loving his Son when he suffered and died on the cross? No! Nothing can ever separate us from the love of God.

JOB 8

Verses 5-7: "But if you pray to God and seek the favor of the Almighty, and if you are pure and live with integrity, he will surely rise up and restore your happy home. And though you started with little, you will end with much."

Reflection:

What hope do the godless have?

What do they have that gives them lasting security?

Although the godly start with little, because we have asked Jesus to be our Lord and Savior, we will end with much. Jesus is our provider, protector, and our security. Our hope of eternal life and heaven is secure. And our confidence is in our salvation and the promises of God found in the Bible.

Our days on earth are like a fleeting shadow, and no matter how tightly we hold the material things in our lives, they will not endure. But God will fill the mouths of his children with laughter, and his faithful servants will overflow with joy!

JOB 9

Verses 33-35: "If only there were a mediator between us, someone who could bring us together. The mediator could make God stop beating me, and I would no longer live in terror of his punishment. Then I could speak to him without fear, but I cannot do that in my own strength."

Reflection:

Job asked, "But how can a person be declared innocent in God's sight?" (verse 2b)

There is one Mediator between God and people. There's one way to be declared innocent before God. There is only One who can bring holy God and sinful man together. His name is Jesus Christ.

Through Jesus, not by our own strength or good deeds, we become children of God. Because of our acceptance of Christ, we can boldly come to our Father's throne of grace—anytime. And since Jesus is our Mediator, we no longer have to live in fear of condemnation.

Believers are innocent in God's eyes. We are justified by the blood of our Lord and Savior, Jesus Christ. And the God of peace will soon crush Satan—the cause of Job's troubles—under our feet.

JOB 10

Verses 10-12: "You guided my conception and formed me in the womb. You clothed me with skin and flesh, and you knit my bones and sinews together. You gave me life and showed me your unfailing love. My life was preserved by your care."

Reflection:

God has been involved in our lives from the very beginning of our existence. From our mother's womb, God has cared for us. The Bible says, "You saw me before I was born. Every day of my life was recorded in your book. Every moment was laid out before a single day had passed." (Psalm 139:16)

Let there be no doubt that life begins at conception, and each life is precious to God who created us in the womb, planned each one of our days, and gave us life.

JOB 11

Verse 13: "If only you would prepare your heart and lift up your hands to him in prayer!"

Reflection:

May you, a follower of Jesus, live in close fellowship with God through daily prayer and repentance of sins.

May your face be bright with innocence and your heart be filled with hope.

May your weakness be replaced with strength, and may your fear be replaced with courage.

May your misery flow away like water and be forgotten.

May your life be brighter than the noonday and may your darkness be as bright as the morning.

May you lie down unafraid and rest in safety because you are loved and protected by God.

And may many people look to you for help because you are clean and pure in your Father's eyes.

JOB 12

Verse 13a: "But true wisdom and power are found in God..."

Reflection:

Strength and wisdom belong to God. He can turn wise judges into fools. He can remove the royal robes of kings and the insight of elders. He can strip priests of their status and leaders of understanding. God can disarm the strong and put people in prison. Yes, both deceivers and deceived are in God's power.

God can stop the rain and turn the land into a desert, or he can release the waters and flood the earth—remember Noah and the ark! As for the nations, God builds them up and expands them. But he can also abandon them and destroy them—and what God destroys cannot be rebuilt.

"For the life of every living thing is in his hand, and the breath of every human being." (verse 10)

JOB 13

Verse 16: "But this is what will save me—I am not godless. If I were, I could not stand before him."

Reflection:

The godless have no hope. They cannot speak directly to the Almighty because he will not hear the prayers of his enemies. They do not fear God even though one day they will stand before his majestic white throne and be judged for their rebellion. The godless will be proved guilty, and they will face eternal consequences for their sin and rejection of Jesus—the One who paid their penalty.

Although the life of the godly is not without trouble, we can speak to God and know that we are not alone, and he hears our prayers. As beloved followers of his Son, we have been adopted into God's family, and our Father loves it when we come to him. Unlike the godless, the godly will stand before the awesome presence of Jesus Christ, and because of his blood, we will be proved innocent. The godly will be saved and rewarded on the day of judgment.

JOB 14

Verse 1a: "How frail is humanity!"

Reflection:

God has decided the length of our lives. He alone knows exactly how long we will live. And no matter how hard we may try to extend the length of our lives, we will not be given a minute longer. Everyone will die at God's appointed time. Compared to eternity, our lives are very short. We pass through this world like a shadow and quickly disappear.

Can the dead live again? Praise God, the answer is "Yes!" Because our spirit is eternal, once our body dies, we will live forever.

When people breathe their last, where are they? Where we live depends on what we do with Jesus before we die. Those who have asked Jesus to be their Savior— whose guilt is covered by his blood—can live with hope during their years of struggle on earth. Because believers have the assurance of spending eternity in heaven, they can eagerly await the release of death. But those who do not know Jesus—whose sins are not forgiven—will experience eternal death, pain, and suffering in hell when they pass from the scene and are sent to the grave.

JOB 15

Verses 32-33: "They will be cut down in the prime of life; their branches will never again be green. They will be like a vine whose grapes are harvested too early, like an olive tree that loses its blossoms before the fruit can form."

Reflection:

The wicked have no fear of God. They conceive trouble and give birth to evil. Therefore, God has stored up years of trouble for them.

The wicked will live in fear, distress, and anguish. They will writhe in pain throughout their lives. The sound of terror will ring in their ears because they know their day of destruction is near. The waists of the wicked will bulge with fat as they fool themselves by trusting in empty riches that will not last—but instead, emptiness will be their reward. They defiantly shake their fists at God, so God will cut them down in the prime of life. The wicked will not escape the darkness when the breath of God destroys them.

JOB 16

Verse 2b: "What miserable comforters you are!"

Reflection:

In response to Eliphaz, Job said, "Won't you ever stop blowing hot air? What makes you keep on talking?" Sometimes, it is better to say very little or nothing to a person experiencing grief. Talking too much does little to comfort people who are suffering. Just a few words of encouragement are more than enough.

Because Job's entire life was shattered, he felt like God hated him. Job was letting his emotions get the best of him. But emotions never initiate, they always respond. The mind thinks, and the emotions respond. That is the divine pattern. So, one key to controlling your emotions is filling your mind with the truth of the Bible. Another key is giving The Comforter—the Holy Spirit—control of your entire being. As you obediently follow him moment-by-moment, the Spirit of God will feed and strengthen your spirit and mind, and then your emotions will follow.

JOB 17

Verse 12:   "These men say that night is day; they claim that darkness is light."

Reflection:

Job's spirit was crushed, and his so-called friends had closed their minds to understanding. Job felt betrayed, mocked, and hopeless. His eyes were swollen from crying. And he said, "...my life is nearly snuffed out. The grave is ready to receive me." (verse 1b)

In the middle of Job's defense of his innocence, he said, "The innocent rise up against the ungodly. The righteous keep moving forward, and those with clean hands become stronger and stronger." (verses 8b-9) Because we live in a world that says darkness is light, may followers of Jesus Christ rise up against the lies of the ungodly. Since we live in a culture that twists the truth, may believers keep their hands clean and look forward to what lies ahead. And though our bodies grow weaker with age, may the spirits of the righteous grow stronger and stronger.

JOB 18

Verses 11-14: "Terrors surround the wicked and trouble them at every step. Hunger depletes their strength, and calamity waits for them to stumble. Disease eats their skin; death devours their limbs. They are torn from the security of their homes and are brought down to the king of terrors."

Reflection:

Who are the wicked? The people who reject Jesus Christ, the Son of God, are the wicked. They will suffer a horrible and terrifying fate. Their proud and confident stride will be shortened. Their roots will dry up, and their branches will wither. Their life will be snuffed out, and they will be thrust into darkness. All memories of the existence of the wicked will fade, and their names will be forgotten.

Jesus said that at the end of the world, "The angels will come and separate the wicked people from the righteous, throwing the wicked into the fiery furnace, where there will be weeping and gnashing of teeth." (Matthew 13: 49b-50)

JOB 19

Verses 25-27: "But as for me, I know that my Redeemer lives, and he will stand upon the earth at last. And after my body has decayed, yet in my body, I will see God! I will see him for myself. Yes, I will see him with my own eyes. I am overwhelmed at the thought!"

Reflection:

As followers of Jesus Christ, we can look forward with eager expectation to his second coming from heaven. Just as Job said, one day, we will see the Son of God as he really is, with perfect clarity. And when Christ appears, we will know everything completely because we will be like him.

When we who believe in Jesus feel stuck in a situation—like God has blocked us from moving—it is important that we don't lose hope. Instead, may we rejoice in our confident hope.

When we see our brothers and sisters in pain, we shouldn't think, "It's their own fault." Rather, may we encourage them to be patient in trouble.

And when we see a suffering Christian, we should not view their sickness as evidence of their sin. But instead, may we keep on praying for them.

JOB 20

Verses 4-7a: "Don't you realize that from the beginning of time, ever since people were first placed on the earth, the triumph of the wicked has been short lived and the joy of the godless has been only temporary? Though the pride of the godless reaches to the heavens and their heads touch the clouds, yet they will vanish forever, thrown away like their own dung."

Reflection:

The reward that the wicked can look forward to from God includes his anger descending on them in torrents, their treasures being thrown into deepest darkness, and a belly full of trouble. The inheritance decreed by God for the wicked is that their wealth will bring them no joy, their prosperity will not endure, and they will be overcome by misery. "They will fade like a dream and not be found. They will vanish like a vision in the night." (verse 8)

JOB 21

Verses 14-15: "And yet they said say to God, 'Go away. We want no part of you and your ways. Who is the Almighty, and why should we obey him? What good will it do us to pray?'"

Reflection:

The wicked fail to recognize that every good thing they have comes from God—family, prosperity, and health. In his mercy, God sometimes allows the wicked to be the picture of good health, growing old and powerful. Because of God's patience, he may spare the ungodly from disaster and grant them prosperity and peace. And in his goodness, God may allow those who reject Jesus to live comfortable and secure lives.

Yet our lives on this earth are very short compared to eternity. For the wicked, this temporary life is the best—the closest thing to heaven—they will ever get to experience. But for those who belong to Christ, this life is the worst it will ever be because the best is yet to come!

JOB 22

Verse 21:   "Submit to God, and you will have peace; then things will go well for you."

Reflection:

In contrast to the wicked, the righteous listen to God's instructions. Because they have repented of their sins and returned to God, he hears the prayers of his beloved children. The godly have repented of their sins and cleaned up their lives. And by believing in Jesus, their relationship with God has been restored.

May we, the children of God, take delight in the Almighty. May our heavenly Father be our greatest treasure, and may we store his Word in our hearts. May God help us to succeed as he lights up the road and shows us the way to go. And because our hands are pure, may God help people in trouble and save sinners when we pray for them.

JOB 23

Verse 10: "But he knows where I am going. And when he tests me, I will come out as pure as gold."

Reflection:

Despite feeling like thick, impenetrable darkness was all around him, Job knew that God was in control. He didn't understand why bad things had happened to him, but Job realized that God controlled his destiny and would do whatever he had planned to do. And although it seemed to Job that God was hidden, he knew in his heart that God was present.

God does allow tests of faith, which conform believers into the likeness of Jesus, in the lives of his children. May we, followers of the Way, not fear bad news and confidently trust in the Lord to care for us. May we always stay on God's path and treasure his Word more than daily food. And when it's finally over, may we be able to say, "When he tested me, I came out as pure as gold."

JOB 24

Verses 15-17a: "The adulterer waits for the twilight, saying, 'No one will see me then.' He hides his face so no one will know him. Thieves break into houses at night and sleep in the daytime. They are not acquainted with the light. The black night is their morning."

Reflection:

Wicked people rebel against the light. They refuse to acknowledge God or live in the light of his ways because "All who do evil hate the light and refuse to go near it for fear their sins will be exposed." (John 3:20) But the Lord is always watching them, and everything they own is cursed.

Evil people live in fear, with no assurance of life. God, in his power, will break them like a tree in a tornado. And since they hate the light, sinners will be consumed by the grave, become a sweet treat for maggots, and spend eternity with the terrors of the darkness.

JOB 25

Verses 5-6:   "God is more glorious than the moon; he shines brighter than the stars. In comparison, people are maggots; we mortals are mere worms."

Reflection:

Words fall short when describing our glorious God, but the Bible gives us a glimpse of him:

In Isaiah 6:1-3, we read, "It was in the year King Uzziah died that I saw the Lord. He was sitting on a lofty throne, and the train of his robe filled the Temple. Attending him were mighty seraphim, each having six wings. With two wings, they covered their faces, with two they covered their feet, and with two, they flew. They were calling out to each other, 'Holy, holy, holy is the Lord of Heaven's Armies! The whole earth is filled with his glory!'"

In Revelation 1:13-16, we learn more about God's glory. "And standing in the middle of the lampstands was someone like the Son of Man. He was wearing a long robe with the gold sash across his chest. His head and his hair were white like wool, as white as snow. And his eyes were like flames of fire. His feet were like polished bronze refined in a furnace, and his voice thundered like mighty ocean waves. He held seven stars in his right hand and a sharp two-edged sword came from his mouth. And his face was like the sun in all its brilliance."

And in Revelation 4:3 the Bible tells us, "The one sitting on the throne was as brilliant as gemstones—like jasper and carnelian. And the glow of an emerald circled his throne like a rainbow."

JOB 26

Verses 11-12a: "The foundations of heaven tremble; they shudder at his rebuke. By his power, the sea grew calm."

Reflection:

Who can comprehend the omnipotence of God? Our all-powerful Father hung the earth on nothing, created the horizons when he separated the waters, and set the boundary between day and night. And these things are merely a whisper of his power!

In Luke 8:23-25, Jesus Christ—God in flesh—gives his disciples a first-hand experience of his power over nature. "As they sailed across, Jesus settled down for a nap. But soon, a fierce storm came down on the lake. The boat was filling with water, and they were in real danger. The disciples went and woke him up, shouting, 'Master, master, we're going to drown!' When Jesus woke up, he rebuked the wind and the raging waves. Suddenly, the storm stopped, and all was calm. Then he asked them, 'Where is your faith?' The disciples were terrified and amazed. 'Who is this man?' they asked each other. 'When he gives a command, even the wind and waves obey him!'"

May we, as disciples of Jesus, be strong in the Lord and in his mighty power. And like the wind and waves were calmed by the voice of Jesus, may we also be still, and know that he is God!

JOB 27

Verse 8: "For what hope do the godless have when God cuts them off and takes away their life?"

Reflection:

When those who reject Jesus Christ die, they cannot call to God. He will not listen to their cry. It's too late. Their situation is hopeless, and their soul is lost forever.

Material wealth is the primary focus of many people. But Jesus asked, "And what do you benefit if you gain the whole world but lose your own soul? Is anything worth more than your soul?" (Matthew 16:26) Jesus also said, "Yes, a person is a fool to store up earthly wealth but not have a rich relationship with God." (Luke 12:21) Because of God's love, Jesus came down from heaven and became poor, so that by his poverty, he could make us spiritually rich.

May God open the eyes of people who do not know his Son as their Savior and Lord. May they believe and receive Jesus into their hearts and lives. And may they become spiritually wealthy and have a rich relationship with God.

JOB 28

Verses 9-12: "People know how to tear apart flinty rocks and overturn the roots of mountains. They cut tunnels in the rocks and uncover precious stones. They dam up the trickling streams and bring to light the hidden treasures. But do people know where to find wisdom? Where can they find understanding?"

Reflection:

Wisdom is not found among the living. It cannot be bought with gold or purchased with silver. Wisdom is more valuable than all the precious jewels in the world. "God alone understands the way to wisdom; he knows where it can be found...And this is what he says to all humanity: 'The fear of the Lord is true wisdom; to forsake evil is real understanding.'" (verses 23, 28)

JOB 29

Verse 2-3: "I long for the years gone by when God took care of me, when he lit up the way before me, and I walked safely through the darkness."

Reflection:

Understandably, Job longed for the days before he lost everything—his children, his possessions, and his health. In those days, he felt God's friendship and presence in his life. Job was honored among the city leaders and respected by everyone. He even assisted the poor and helped the orphans. Job was an honest, righteous man, and people listened to his advice.

Although Job may not have felt the Lord's presence in his suffering, God said, "I will never fail you. I will never abandon you." (Hebrews 13:5b) Since all of God's promises are true, we know that Job's good deeds were not done in vain and that he was not abandoned by the Lord who could see his innocence.

Even though it is impossible for people to understand God's ways, may we know that his promises are true. May we trust that his way is perfect and that he will make our way perfect, too. And may we believe that God sees us, and he will reward his children for doing right.

JOB 30

Verse 28a: "I walk in gloom, without sunlight."

Reflection:

Mocked. Taunted. Despised. These are some of the words that Job used to describe how he was being treated by others. Job not only suffered physical pain, but he also suffered from mental anguish and depression. And it's no wonder, since he felt like he had no one to help him—not even God.

When we feel like Job, may we stand firm against the schemes of the devil and be strong in our faith. May we remember that believers all over the world are enduring suffering. And may we remind ourselves of God's promise: "Don't be afraid, for I am with you. Don't be discouraged, for I am your God. I will strengthen you and help you. I will hold you up with my victorious right hand." (Isaiah 41:10)

JOB 31

Verse 35b: "Let the Almighty answer me. Let my accuser write out the charges against me."

Reflection:

Search your heart for the answers to Job's questions:

➢ Have I lied to anyone or deceived anyone?

➢ Have I strayed from God's pathway?

➢ Have I lusted for what my eyes have seen?

➢ Have I treated people unfairly?

➢ Have I refused to help the poor?

➢ Have I been stingy and refused to share?

➢ Have I put my trust and security in money?

➢ Have I gloated about my wealth?

➢ Have I been enticed to worship anything other than God?

➢ Have I rejoiced when harm or disaster struck my enemies?

➢ Have I turned away a person in need?

➢ Have I tried to hide my sins?

➢ Have I feared people and kept quiet when I should have spoken up?

Dear Heavenly Father,

You are my God and my Creator. You see everything I do and every step I take. Have mercy on me. Forgive me for all my sins—past, present, and future—by the cleansing power of the blood of your Son, Jesus Christ. Amen

JOB 32

Verse 8: "But there is a spirit within people, the breath of the Almighty within them, that makes them intelligent."

Reflection:

Elihu was younger than Job's three friends, so he listened and waited until they were done speaking before he told everyone what he thought. Elihu said, "For I am full of pent-up words, and the spirit within me urges me on...I must speak to find relief, so let me give my answers." (verses 18 and 20)

Just because a person is older doesn't always mean they are wiser, especially if they are ungodly. But the Holy Spirit, who lives in God's children, gives them wisdom. So we, whom God has united with Christ Jesus (who is wisdom itself), are encouraged to ask him if we need wisdom, knowledge, and understanding. And when we are in tune with the Spirit, he will tell us when to remain quiet and when we must speak.

JOB 33

Verse 14: "For God speaks again and again, though people do not recognize it."

Reflection:

God is always speaking. But most people do not have spiritual ears to hear him or spiritual eyes to see him. God speaks in dreams and visions. He whispers in people's ears and makes them turn from doing wrong. God speaks when he disciplines people—sometimes with pain and sickness. But he also speaks when he rescues them from the grave and restores their life.

God speaks to us when we read his Word, the Bible. Through Scripture, we learn about God's love and character. He warns us about sin, teaches us how to live an abundant life, and shows us how to go to heaven and have eternal life through his Son, Jesus Christ. You may refuse to listen to people, but be careful that you do not refuse to listen to God, who speaks to you from heaven.

JOB 34

Verse 10: "Listen to me, you who have understanding. Everyone knows that God doesn't sin! The Almighty can do no wrong."

Reflection:

Who are people to condemn the Almighty? God watches how everyone lives and sees everything they do. In his justice, he strikes down the wicked, whether they are rich or poor. It doesn't matter how great a person may be in the world's eyes—God made us all. And it's in him that we live and move and exist.

Think about this: "If God were to take back his spirit and withdraw his breath, *all* life would cease, and humanity would turn again to dust." (verse 14) People who show no respect and say angry words against God are talking out of ignorance. If they reject God's Son, that's their choice. But Jesus will be their judge—whether they accept him or not—and he will decide their penalty.

JOB 35

Verse 6: "If you sin, how does that affect God? Even if you sin again and again, what effect will it have on him?"

Reflection:

People's sins do not affect God. They only hurt themselves and those around them. But even though our sins can't hurt God, he is concerned because he loves us and knows the suffering that eternity holds for unrepentant sinners.

Similarly, our good deeds are no great gift to God our Creator. As sinners saved by God's grace, we owe him everything. And we are unworthy servants who have simply done our duty when we serve our Master obediently by doing what he tells us in his Word.

May people swallow their pride and repent of their sins. May God forgive them and answer them when they cry out to him in prayer. May God's children serve him with a humble heart of love. And may our Father give us patience to wait for him to bring justice, and confidence to know that he will.

JOB 36

Verses 16-17: "God is leading you away from danger, Job, to a place free from distress. He is setting your table with the best food. But you are obsessed with whether the godless will be judged. Don't worry, judgment and justice will be upheld."

Reflection:

God is mighty in power and understanding. If the innocent are bound in chains of trouble, he shows them why. God gets their attention through adversity, shows them their sins of pride, and commands that they turn from evil. So, by their suffering, God rescues those who suffer.

But God does not let the wicked live. Because the godless are full of pride and resentment, they will not ask God for help or turn back from evil, even when he punishes them. As a result, many who reject God will cross over the river of death when they are young, after wasting their lives in immoral living.

May people listen and obey God. May they be blessed with prosperity. And may all their years be pleasant.

JOB 37

Verses 23a: "We cannot imagine the power of the Almighty..."

Reflection:

How powerful is God? Just consider how he controls the weather. God directs the snow to fall and the rain to pour. He sends the wind, cold, and ice. With wonderful perfection and skill, God commands the clouds to do whatever he wants them to.

The Almighty is clothed in dazzling splendor that is brighter than the sun. His voice is glorious as it roars from his mouth in the rolling thunder. And everyone watches God's power when his lightning flashes in the sky.

We can't even imagine the greatness of God's power! All who are wise will fear him and show him reverence.

JOB 38

Verses 1-3: "Then the Lord answered Job from the whirlwind: 'Who is this that questions my wisdom with such ignorant words? Brace yourself like a man, because I have some questions for you, and you must answer them.'"

Reflection:

Sometimes, people question God's wisdom and talk about him without any knowledge of whom they are speaking. When we think that we are smarter than God, we would do well to answer God's questions to Job:

➤ "Where were you when I laid the foundations of the earth?" (verse 4a)

➤ "Who kept the sea inside its boundaries?" (verse 8a)

➤ "Have you ever commanded the morning to appear and caused the dawn to rise in the east?" (verse 12)

➤ "Do you know where the gates of death are located?" (verse 17a)

➤ "Can you direct the movement of the stars?" (verse 31a)

➤ "Do you know the laws of the universe? Can you use them to regulate the earth?" (verse 33)

➤ "Can you make lightning appear and cause it to strike as you direct?" (verse 35)

➤ "Who gives intuition to the heart and instinct to the mind?" (verse 36)

JOB 39

Verses 19-20: "Have you given the horse its strength or clothed its neck with a flowing mane? Did you give it the ability to leap like a locust? Its majestic snorting is terrifying!"

Reflection:

God is the Creator and Controller of the entire universe, including the animal kingdom. God watches over the wild goats and deer as they give birth. God untied the ropes of the wild donkey and gave the wild ox its strength. God deprived the ostrich of wisdom but gave her speed to pass the swiftest horse. God makes the hawk soar and causes the eagle to build its nest in the highest heights.

Psalm 36:6 says, "Your righteousness is like the mighty mountains, your justice like the ocean depths. You care for people and animals alike, O Lord." May we ponder the many unique animals that God has made, be amazed by his creativity, and remember that God cares for each one—just like he cares for you and me.

JOB 40

Verses 1-2: "Then the Lord said to Job, 'Do you still want to argue with the Almighty? You are God's critic, but do you have the answers?'"

Reflection:

People criticize God for the calamity he sends and the circumstances he allows. They discredit his justice and condemn his decisions. They think God enjoys hurting people and causing them sorrow. But who are we—the created—to argue with our Creator about his holy and mysterious ways? Are we as wise and strong as our omniscient and omnipotent God?

May we humble ourselves and respond to the Most High like Job, "I am nothing—how could I ever find the answers? I will cover my mouth with my hand. I have said too much already. I have nothing more to say." (verses 4-5)

JOB 41

Verse 11: "Who has given me anything that I need to pay back? Everything under heaven is mine."

Reflection:

"The earth is the Lord's, and everything in it. The world and all its people belong to him." (Psalm 24:1). God owes us nothing—we owe him everything. But despite God's goodness, people still choose to sinfully rebel and disobey him. And God still has mercy on us. In fact, God loves us so much that he gave his one and only Son, Jesus, so that everyone who believes in him will have eternal life.

God's knowledge is limitless, making it impossible for us to understand his decisions. And since everything comes from God, belongs to God, and exists by God's power, who are we to question his wisdom and ways? Job's encounter with God humbled him. May we take his example to heart and approach God with humility, respect, and reverence. All glory to God forever and ever!

JOB 42

Verse 10: "When Job prayed for his friends, the Lord restored his fortunes. In fact, the Lord gave him twice as much as before!"

Reflection:

Job saw the Lord with his own eyes, took back everything he said, and sat in dust and ashes to show his repentance. Job's friends offered sacrifices to God for the inaccurate things they had said about him. And after Job prayed for Eliphaz, Bildad, and Zophar, God restored Job's fortunes, family, and friends. So God doubled Job's blessings in the second half of his life, and he died an old man who had lived a long, full life!

"For no one is abandoned by the Lord forever. Though he brings grief, he also shows compassion because of the greatness of his unfailing love." (Lamentations 3:31-32)

✧ ✧ ✧

The Book of
Psalms

PSALM 1

Verse 6: "For the Lord watches over the path of the godly, but the path of the wicked leads to destruction."

Reflection:

There are only two paths in life. Which one will you choose?

> The path of the godly leads to joy. The godly delight in meditating on God's Word. Like green trees planted by living water, the godly bear good fruit in each season of their lives. And because the Lord watches over the godly, they prosper in all they do.

> The path of the wicked leads to destruction. The wicked are like worthless chaff. They are sinful mockers of Jesus Christ, his followers, and the Bible. And at the time of judgment, they will be condemned.

"He is ready to separate the chaff from the wheat with his winnowing fork. Then he will clean up the threshing area, gathering the wheat into his barn but burning the chaff with never-ending fire." (Luke 3:17)

PSALM 2

Verses 1-3: "Why are the nations so angry? Why do they waste their time with futile plans? The kings of the earth prepare for battle; the rulers plot together against the Lord and against his anointed one. 'Let us break their chains' they cry, 'and free ourselves from slavery to God.'"

Reflection:

God, the Father, has anointed Jesus Christ, his Son, as the eternal King. Jesus is now ruling from heaven. But one day, he will rule from Jerusalem.

The whole earth belongs to King Jesus. So submit to God's royal Son and serve him with reverent fear. For all who take refuge in Jesus will experience true freedom and joy. But those who reject Christ, plot to fight against him, and ignore God's warnings will—in the end—be destroyed with his fierce fury.

PSALM 3

Verses 1-3: "O Lord, I have so many enemies; so many are against me. So many are saying, 'God will never rescue him!' But you, O Lord are a shield around me; you are my glory, the one who holds my head high."

Reflection:

Whether we have many enemies or many problems, may the Lord watch over those who belong to him.

Because God is our shield, may Christians not be afraid in any circumstance.

When we call out to our Savior in prayer, may he answer us from his holy heaven.

And when we lay down to sleep, may God's children slumber safely under the watchful eyes of Jesus.

"Victory comes from you, O Lord. May you bless your people." (verse 8)

PSALM 4

Verse 3: "You can be sure of this: The Lord set apart the godly for himself. The Lord will answer when I call to him."

Reflection:

O God, who declares me innocent, hear my prayer:

How long until you free me from my troubles? How long until you answer my prayers? How long?

Have mercy on me, Lord, and let your face smile on me. Keep me safe from liars. And help me not to sin by letting anger control me.

Enable me to trust you to take care of everything and lead me to better times of abundant harvest. Because you have set me apart for yourself, I will lie down and sleep in peace. Then, in the morning, I will awake to great joy!

In the name of Jesus Christ, Amen

Read PSALM 5

Verse 8: "Lead me in the right path, O Lord, or my enemies will conquer me. Make your way plain for me to follow."

Reflection:

Because God's path is the right path—the best path—for us to follow, this psalm of David should be the prayer of every follower of Jesus. Because we love Jesus, we want to make sure that we are living each moment according to his will. And because Christ blesses the godly, he will surround us with his shield of love and make his way clear for us to follow when we surrender our life to him and obey him.

Like David, may we bring our requests to the Lord each morning and wait expectantly. And rather than trying to make things happen in our own strength, may we slow down and wait patiently for Jesus to reveal the next step.

57

PSALM 6

Verses 2-3: "Have compassion on me, Lord, for I am weak. Heal me, Lord, for my bones are in agony. I am sick at heart. How long, O Lord, until you restore me?"

Reflection:

Have you ever felt like David—weak, in need of healing, or sick at heart? It is difficult to go through these things. And like David, we can get tired of waiting for the Lord to restore us, and we ask him, "How long, Lord?"

God has a purpose for your waiting, and while he is working, our Father wants his children to be confident in hope, patient in trouble, and to keep on praying. The Lord does hear your plea for help, and because of his unfailing love, he will answer your prayer.

PSALM 7

Verses 14-16: "The wicked conceive evil; they are pregnant with trouble and give birth to lies. They dig a deep pit to trap others, then fall into it themselves. The trouble they make for others backfires on them. The violence they plan falls on their own heads."

Reflection:

God is an honest judge. The righteous sing praise to the Lord Most High and thank him because he is just! He rules over the nations from on high. He looks deep within a person's mind and heart and knows if they are guilty of sin. And God knows who his enemies are— those who reject Jesus Christ and thereby reject him.

God is a shield. He protects those who belong to him. He rescues those who are declared innocent of sin because they have accepted his gift of salvation through Jesus, his Son.

God is righteous. He will end the evil of the wicked, but he defends the righteous. God is angry with the wicked every day, but he saves those whose hearts are true and right.

PSALM 8

Verse 1:   "O Lord, our Lord, your majestic name fills the earth! Your glory is higher than the heavens."

Reflection:

God's glory towers over the heavens, and his majesty fills the earth. When we look at the sky, we can see God's glory in the sun, moon, and stars. The work of his hands can also be seen in the animals, birds, and fish. "Let every created thing give praise to the Lord, for he issued his command, and they came into being." (Psalm 148:5)

God made everything, but the thing he created that he loves the most is you and me. God thinks about us and cares for us so much that he sent Jesus so that we can believe in him and be with him forever.

The earth that God made is truly amazing, but imagine what we will witness when, one day, we enter his glorious heaven!

PSALM 9

Verse 17:   "The wicked will go down to the grave. This is the fate of all the nations who ignore God."

Reflection:

When people and nations defy God, it may seem like he lets them get away with it—but not for long. God is known for his righteous justice, and people will eventually be punished for their wicked deeds. They will know that they are merely human.

God avenges murder, cares for the helpless, shelters the oppressed, and hears the cries of those who suffer. He does not abandon those who belong to him and have trusted in Jesus for salvation. The Lord shows mercy to the godly and fills them with joy. But he fairly executes judgment from his throne, destroying both wicked people and nations who ignore him.

PSALM 10

Verse 4:   "The wicked are too proud to seek God. They seem to think that God is dead."

Reflection:

The wicked think that nothing bad will ever happen to them. They despise God. Their mouths are full of lies and cursing—even cursing the Lord Jesus Christ. The wicked think that God isn't watching them, but God is not blind, and he has not closed his eyes. He sees everything they do!

God sees the trouble and grief caused by the wicked, and he takes note of their evil thoughts, words, and deeds. The wicked are blind and do not see the punishment awaiting them when the living God calls them to account, and justice is served.

PSALM 11

Verse 1a: "I trust in the Lord for protection."

Reflection:

The world tells us, "Trust yourself. Protect yourself. Run to the mountains for safety." But this is not the way of the godly. We trust in the Lord for protection. The Lord Jesus is in his holy Temple, ruling over everything from heaven. He is closely watching every person on earth—the righteous and the wicked alike.

God hates the wicked. They shoot from the shadows at those whose hearts are right. They attack the foundations of law and order. They seek to twist the truth and destroy justice. What can the righteous do? Trust God for protection.

God will punish the wicked with blazing coals, burning sulfur, and scorching winds. But the virtuous will see the face of Jesus Christ, their Savior. This is the righteous justice of the Lord.

PSALM 12

Verse 8: "...even though the wicked strut about, and evil is praised throughout the land."

Reflection:

Even though the wicked strut about, the Lord will silence their boastful tongues.

Even though evil is praised throughout the land, the Lord sees the violence done to the poor and helpless.

Even though the godly are fast disappearing, the Lord will forever preserve his children.

Even though neighbors lie and deceive each other, the Lord's promises are pure.

Even though the wicked say, "Who can stop us?" The Lord replies, "Now I will rise up!"

Even though the faithful will one day vanish from the earth, it's because the Lord has rescued them as they have longed for him to do.

PSALM 13

Verses 1-2: "O Lord, how long will you forget me? Forever? How long will you look the other way? How long must I struggle with anguish in my soul, with sorrow in my heart every day? How long will my enemy have the upper hand?"

Reflection:

Most of us have asked God, "How long?" at some point in our lives. We get weary of living in difficult situations and yearn to be rescued and restored by our heavenly Father.

The key to waiting is, "But I will trust." (verse 5a) We can be assured that God will act on our behalf because of his unfailing love for us. And, like David the psalmist, we will rejoice and sing to the Lord with a sparkle in our eyes because of his goodness to us.

PSALM 14

Verse 1a: "Only fools say in their hearts, 'There is no God.'"

Reflection:

The Bible describes fools as people who wouldn't think of praying to the Lord. Because they deny the existence of God, they have replaced the true God with the god of self. They, not Jesus, sit on the throne of their life. But one day—hopefully before it's too late—terror will grip them, and they will realize how foolish they have been.

At one point, we all, the entire human race, turned away from God and lived as fools—corrupt and evil. But the truly wise will seek God. Just as building a house without a good foundation is foolish, trying to build your life with yourself as the foundation is foolish.

May those who say there is no God come to know God. For there is no God but Jehovah in all of heaven and earth.

PSALM 15

Verse 1: "Who may worship in your sanctuary, Lord? Who may enter your presence on your holy hill?"

Reflection:

Those who belong to God through Jesus Christ may enter his presence and worship him—now and forever.

As believers who are sanctified by the power of the Holy Spirit, may we be people who live blameless lives, do what is right, speak the truth from sincere hearts, refuse to gossip or speak evil, and not harm others.

May God's children despise flagrant sinners, honor the faithful followers of the Lord, and keep our promises—even when it hurts.

May believers be generous and unable to lie.

And as we are transformed and become more like Jesus in character, conduct, and conversation, may God's people stand firm forever.

PSALM 16

Verse 8: "I know the Lord is always with me. I will not be shaken, for he is right beside me."

Reflection:

Believers in Jesus Christ—the true children of God—can claim all the wonderful promises in the Bible, including all the good things found in this Psalm:

- ➢ God is my refuge, keeping me eternally safe.
- ➢ The Lord is my cup of blessing, giving me a heavenly inheritance.
- ➢ God fills my heart with gladness, letting me rest in safety.
- ➢ The Lord guides and guards me, instructing my heart even at night.
- ➢ The Lord is my Master, giving me every good thing.
- ➢ God himself shows me the way of life, giving me the joy of his presence!

PSALM 17

Verses 1-2: "O Lord, hear my plea for justice. Listen to my cry for help. Pay attention to my prayer, for it comes from honest lips. Declare me innocent, for you see those who do right."

Reflection:

May God answer the prayers of the righteous. May he bend down and listen when the godly talk to him. And may our Father show his children unfailing love in wonderful ways.

May the Lord protect us from cruel and wicked people who look to the world for their reward. May he guard us from our enemies. May he rescue us from evil by his mighty power. And may we, his treasured ones, be satisfied when we see Jesus face to face.

PSALM 18

Verses 1-2: "I love you, Lord; you are my strength. The Lord is my rock, my fortress, and my savior; my God is my rock, in whom I find protection. He is my shield, the power that saves me, and my place of safety."

Reflection:

David began this Psalm with the words, "I love you, Lord." This is the key to everything. By loving God and putting him first in your life, he will care for you like he cared for David. From his sanctuary, the Most High will hear your prayers for help, and answer. He will save and protect, shield and support, rescue and reward you.

By following God's perfect way, your way will be perfect. He will reach down from heaven and keep you from slipping. The Lord will lead you to safety, light up your darkness, and arm you with strength for daily spiritual battle. Your enemies will not stand a chance, as the living God will pay back those who harm you. But the God of our salvation will give unfailing love and great victory to those who belong to his Son, Jesus Christ!

PSALM 19

Verse 14:   "May the words of my mouth and the meditation of my heart be pleasing to you, O Lord, my rock and my redeemer."

Reflection:

Meditation on Scripture, which is trustworthy and true, will transform your heart and mind and be evident in your thoughts, words, actions, and attitudes.

Confession of sin to the Lord—known and unknown—will cleanse your heart, keep sin from controlling you, and give you freedom from guilt.

Obeying God's Word, which is right and clear, will result in a great reward.

Reading the Bible, which is pure and perfect, will revive your soul, give you wisdom and warning, bring joy to your heart, and give you insight for living.

PSALM 20

Verse 7: "Some nations boast of their chariots and horses, but we boast in the name of the Lord our God."

Reflection:

Some people boast of their cars, houses, and material things that are temporary. But children of God can eternally boast in Jesus Christ our Savior, God Almighty our Father, and the Holy Spirit within us.

To be blessed is to be fully satisfied and to thrive on the inside even when life is falling apart on the outside. Those who delight in the Lord Jesus will be blessed with God-given safety, help, strength, success, answered prayers, and victory. So don't be envious of people who don't belong to Jesus. Like nations who turn their backs on God, they will fall and collapse, but those who boast in the name of the Lord Jesus Christ will rise up and stand firm.

PSALM 21

Verses 6-7: "You have endowed him with eternal blessings and given him the joy of your presence. For the king trusts in the Lord. The unfailing love of the Most High will keep him from stumbling."

Reflection:

When we trust in Jesus, may his unfailing love keep us from stumbling.

When we rejoice in Jesus, may he give us victory.

When we put Jesus first, may he give us our heart's desire.

When we withhold nothing from Jesus, may he withhold nothing we request.

When we give our heart and life to Jesus, may he give us the joy of his presence and eternal blessings.

PSALM 22

Verse 1a: "My God, my God, why have you abandoned me?"

Reflection:

Throughout the Bible, which was written by Holy Spirit-inspired men, Jesus is revealed to us. This prophetic Psalm pictures the crucifixion of the Messiah.

"My God, my God, why have you abandoned me?" (verse 1a) These are the words spoken by Jesus on the cross. See Mark 15:34.

"Is this the one who relies on the Lord? Then let the Lord save him! If the Lord loves him so much, let the Lord rescue him!" (verse 8) The people and religious leaders mocked and shouted words like this at Jesus when he was crucified.

"My life is poured out like water, and all my bones are out of joint. My heart is like wax, melting within me. My strength has dried up like sun baked clay. My tongue sticks to the roof of my mouth." (verse 14-15a) These words picture Christ as he hung on the cross.

"They have pierced my hands and feet. I can count all my bones. My enemies stare at me and gloat. They divide my garments among themselves and throw dice for my clothing." (verse 16b-18) Again, this prophesied what would happen to Jesus, which was fulfilled in Mark 15:24.

To pay for our sins and offer salvation to all people, Jesus offered his body and shed his blood as our sacrificial Lamb on the cross. And to all who repent and ask him into their heart, Jesus offers forgiveness of sins and everlasting life. Please pray and accept God's gift of salvation now.

PSALM 23

Verse 1a: "The Lord is my shepherd."

Reflection:

Jesus Christ is the Good Shepherd who sacrificed his life for the sheep. Have you accepted Jesus as your Shepherd—or are you still a lost sheep? If Jesus is your Shepherd, you know him, listen to him, and follow him. Only then can you claim all the promises found in the Bible, including Psalm 23.

In Jesus, the Good Shepherd, I have *all* that I need:

➤ He gives me rest.
➤ He leads me to his peace.
➤ He renews my strength.
➤ He guides me along the right path.
➤ He is always close beside me, so I will not be afraid.
➤ He protects and comforts me.
➤ He prepares a feast for me.
➤ He honors and blesses me.
➤ He gives me his unfailing love and goodness.
➤ He lets me live with him in his house forever.

PSALM 24

Verses 1-2: "The earth is the Lord's, and everything in it. The world and all its people belong to him. For he laid the earth's foundation on the seas and built it on the ocean depths."

Reflection:

Even though the world and all its people belong to God, not all people may stand in God's holy place. Only those whose hands and hearts have been purified from sin by the blood of Jesus Christ will receive the Lord's blessing and have a right relationship with God.

Only those who have accepted Jesus as their Savior may seek God in prayer and worship in his presence. Only those who belong to Jesus will be protected by the King of Glory—The Lord of Heaven's Armies—strong and mighty, invincible in battle.

PSALM 25

Verses 1-2a: "O Lord, I give my life to you. I trust in you, my God!"

Reflection:

In these words, we learn how to live in Christ:

➤ "O Lord, I give my life to you." (verse 1)

- First, give your life to Christ by receiving him as your Lord and Savior.

➤ "I trust in you, my God!" (verse 2a)

- Trust in Jesus to take care of you and everything that touches your life.

➤ "All day long, I put my hope in you." (verse 5b)

- Put your hope in the Lord—don't give up.

➤ "My eyes are always on the Lord." (verse 15a)

- Focus on God—his presence, his love, his wisdom, his power, his faithfulness—and eternal things.

➤ "In you, I take refuge." (verse 20b)

- When Satan whispers thoughts of worry, fear, or discouragement, take refuge in Jesus. Go to him in prayer, give him your cares, and receive peace of mind and heart in Christ.

PSALM 26

Verse 12a: "Now I stand on solid ground."

Reflection:

We, too, can stand on solid ground and praise the Lord when, like David, we act with integrity.

When we trust in the Lord without wavering, we are on solid ground.

When we are always aware of God's unfailing love and live according to his truth, we stand on solid ground.

When we do not spend time with liars, do not go along with hypocrites, hate the gatherings of those who do evil, and refuse to join in with the wicked, we are standing on solid ground.

When we love to go to God's house to sing and worship him, we are on solid ground.

And when we come to Jesus, listen to his teachings, and obey him, we are standing firm on solid ground.

PSALM 27

Verse 1: "The Lord is my light and my salvation—so why should I be afraid? The Lord is my fortress, protecting me from danger, so why should I tremble?"

Reflection:

Children of God, who belong to Jesus, are filled with the light of the Holy Spirit. Those who do not have the light, who do not belong to Jesus, are enemies of God and will often attack him by attacking his children. But even when we are attacked, we can remain confident and unafraid because the Lord will never abandon us.

When accusations and threats come, we must be brave and courageous and wait patiently for the Lord to act. Our enemies and foes will stumble and fall, but we will not fall into their hands. For God will place us out of their reach, and we will see the Lord's mercy and goodness.

PSALM 28

Verse 7: "The Lord is my strength and shield. I trust him with all my heart. He helps me, and my heart is filled with joy. I burst out in songs of thanksgiving."

Reflection:

May the Lord give you moment-by-moment strength. May he protect and shield you from wicked people who speak friendly words but plan evil in their hearts. May you trust Jesus with all your heart and receive his peace.

May you realize that nothing is too big or too small to take to the Lord in prayer—he cares about everything that touches your life. May your heart be filled with joy as you see God answer your cries for help. And may you burst out and praise him with songs of gratitude!

May the Good Shepherd lead you and help you every day. And may he bless you and carry you in his arms forever.

PSALM 29

Verses 1, 9b: "Honor the Lord, you heavenly beings; honor the Lord for his glory and strength...In his Temple everyone shouts, 'Glory!'"

Reflection:

The God of Glory is powerful and majestic. He rules over the floodwaters. With his voice, he creates earthquakes that shake the wilderness. He strikes with tree-splitting bolts of lightning. God's thunder echoes his strength and holiness over the sea. And in tornadoes, the Lord twists the mighty oaks and strips the forests bare.

The God of Glory reigns as king forever. And even during storms, he gives his people strength and blesses them with peace. So honor the Lord for the glory of his name and worship him for the splendor of his holiness.

PSALM 30

Verse 5b: "Weeping may last through the night, but joy comes with the morning."

Reflection:

We all have dark times—the night—in our lives. Times of illness, death, weeping, and mourning. But for the children of God, the night is only temporary, because we have received the favor, security, and salvation of God through our Lord Jesus Christ.

On earth, God shows us his mercy and faithfulness. He rescues the godly, and we praise his holy name.

Our enemies will not triumph over us.

When we die, we will immediately go to heaven to be with the Lord. There will be no more death or sorrow or crying or pain. Our mourning will be replaced with joyful dancing!

Death will not triumph over us.

And when Jesus returns, he will resurrect our bodies from the grave and transform them into eternal bodies, like his. We will sing praises and give thanks to the Lord our God forever!

The grave will not triumph over us.

PSALM 31

Verse 24: "So be strong and courageous, all you who put your hope in the Lord!"

Reflection:

Why should born-again children of God be strong and courageous?

- ➤ Because God is a faithful God who does what is right.
- ➤ Because his love is unfailing.
- ➤ Because Christ sees our troubles and cares about the anguish of our soul.
- ➤ Because the Lord lavishes goodness upon those who fear him.
- ➤ Because Jesus blesses those who trust in him— before the watching world.
- ➤ Because our Savior safely hides us, his followers, in the shelter of his presence.
- ➤ Because God answers our calls for help and protects those who are loyal to him.
- ➤ Because our Father holds our future in his hands and lets his favor shine on the godly.

PSALM 32

Verses 1-2: "Oh, what joy for those whose disobedience is forgiven, whose sin is put out of sight! Yes, what joy for those whose record the Lord has cleared of guilt, whose lives are lived in complete honesty!"

Reflection:

When people live in sin and disobedience to God, it affects their spirit, mind, and body. The guilt of unconfessed sin is manifested physically as people waste away and their strength evaporates. Rebellion against God can also be evident when people groan all day because of the Lord's heavy hand and the many sorrows he allows to come their way. But when people finally confess their sins to the Lord Jesus, he forgives them, and the heavy weight of guilt is gone!

In contrast to people living in disobedience to God, those who are his obedient children can rest assured that the Lord himself will guide them, advise them, and watch over them. "So rejoice in the Lord and be glad, all you who obey him! Shout for joy, all you whose hearts are pure!" (verse 11)

PSALM 33

Verse 8:   "Let the whole world fear the Lord, and let everyone stand in awe of him."

Reflection:

Our God is awesome, and he does amazing things! Our Creator merely spoke the word and the heavens were created, the stars were born, and the world began.

God's plans stand firm forever, and we can trust everything he does. Our King looks down from his throne and observes everyone—even you—on earth. He understands our hearts because he made them!

God forgives our sins, rescues us from death, and watches over those who belong to his Son. Our Father is our shield, our help, and our only hope—and he surrounds us with his unfailing love.

In response to our Creator, King, and Father, "Let the godly sing for joy to the Lord; it is fitting for the pure to praise him." (verse 1)

PSALM 34

Verse 8: "Taste and see that the Lord is good. Oh, the joys of those who take refuge in him!"

Reflection:

Praise and prayer are fundamental practices for the children of God.

"I will praise the Lord at all times. I will constantly speak his praises." (verse 1) Like David, may the people of God praise him at all times, boasting only in him and telling of his greatness. May those who take refuge in God praise him for saving, guarding, surrounding, and defending them. May those who serve God praise him for his goodness and provision. And may those who trust in the Lord lack no good thing!

"I prayed to the Lord, and he answered me." (verse 4a) Like David, may the godly pray when they feel fearful, and may God answer by freeing them from their fear. May the righteous pray to God when they need help, and may his ears be open to their cries. May those who fear God pray when they feel desperate and are facing troubles, and may the Lord listen and come to the rescue each time. May those who do right pray when they are brokenhearted and know that the Holy Spirit is close as he comforts them. And may those who look to God for help in prayer experience his goodness and be radiant with joy!

PSALM 35

Verse 1: "O Lord, oppose those who oppose me. Fight those who fight against me."

Reflection:

Who hasn't felt like asking God to defend them against their enemies? It's okay, ask him. God loves justice, and he will fight for his dear children.

> ➢ When people try to harm us, God will humiliate them.
> ➢ When people set a trap for us, they will be caught in it.
> ➢ When people plot against us, God will protect us.
> ➢ When people pursue us, the angel of the Lord will pursue them.
> ➢ When people fight against us, God will blow them away like chaff in the wind.
> ➢ When people maliciously accuse us of things we know nothing about, God will make their path dark and slippery.
> ➢ When people try to kill us, God will send sudden ruin and destruction upon them.

May we rejoice in the Lord who comes to our defense and gives us victory. May we be glad because God delights in blessing his people with peace. And with every bone in our body, may we praise the Lord because no one compares to him!

PSALM 36

Verses 5-6a: "Your unfailing love, O Lord, is as vast as the heavens; your faithfulness reaches beyond the clouds. Your righteousness is like the mighty mountains, your justice like the ocean depths."

Reflection:

God's unfailing love means that he loves all humanity so much that he sent his only Son, Jesus Christ, to die for our sins so that we can have eternal life by believing in him. God's faithfulness means that he will always do what he promises. God's righteousness means that he will always do what is right and best. And God's justice means that those who make no attempt to turn from evil, and have no fear of God at all, will be thrown down—never to rise again.

PSALM 37

Verses 18,23: "Day by day the Lord takes care of the innocent, and they will receive an inheritance that lasts forever...The Lord directs the steps of the godly. He delights in every detail of their lives."

Reflection:

Considering all that our loving Lord Jesus does for us, how should we respond?

> ➤ "Don't worry about the wicked or envy those who do wrong." (verse 1)
> ➤ "Trust in the Lord and do good." (verse 3a)
> ➤ "Take delight in the Lord." (verse 4a)
> ➤ "Commit everything you do to the Lord." (verse 5a)
> ➤ "Be still in the presence of the Lord and wait patiently for him to act." (verse 7a)
> ➤ "Stop being angry! Turn from your rage! Don't lose your temper." (verse 8a)
> ➤ "Put your hope in the Lord and travel steadily along his path." (verse 34a)

PSALM 38

Verses 1-3: "O Lord, don't rebuke me in your anger or discipline me in your rage! Your arrows have struck deep, and your blows are crushing me. Because of your anger, my whole body is sick; my health is broken because of my sins."

Reflection:

Living with unconfessed sin is bad for your health, and it can make your whole body sick. Guilt from sin is a heavy burden to bear and it can lead to festering wounds, a body racked with constant pain, being filled with grief, a raging fever, an anguished heart, failing strength, wild heartbeats, losing eyesight, groaning, exhaustion, and being completely crushed.

So, what is a person to do with their sins? Do just as David said, "But I confess my sins; I am deeply sorry for what I have done." (verse 18)

PSALM 39

Verse 4: "Lord, remind me how brief my time on earth will be. Remind me that my days are numbered—how fleeting my life is."

Reflection:

Compared to eternity, our lifetime is just a moment. Our time on earth is but a breath in God's eyes. We never know when our last day will be—it could be today. If it is, are you ready for eternity? Where will you spend it?

God says that all our busy rushing and heaping up wealth ends in nothing. Our only hope is in Jesus. So slow down and spend some time thinking about eternity. Get right with God by inviting Jesus into your heart. Repent of your sin and start living for heaven today. Like our ancestors before us, we are just travelers—God's guests—passing through this temporary world. Our life is no longer than the width of our hand, then we are gone and exist no more.

PSALM 40

Verse 5: "O Lord my God, you have performed many wonders for us. Your plans for us are too numerous to list. You have no equal. If I tried to recite all your wonderful deeds, I would never come to the end of them."

Reflection:

When we cry out to God for help, he will replace our pit of despair with a hymn of praise.

When we trust Jesus to take care of all our troubles, he will not hold back his tender mercies.

When we wait patiently for the Lord to help us, many will see and be amazed at what he does.

When we take joy in doing God's will, we can't keep it to ourselves.

When we are not afraid to speak out about God's unfailing love and saving power, those who are searching for him will be filled with joy and gladness.

And when we love God's salvation and faithfulness, we will repeatedly shout, "The Lord is great!"

PSALM 41

Verse 4,10a: "O Lord," I prayed, "have mercy on me. Heal me, for I have sinned against you. Lord, have mercy on me. Make me well again…"

Reflection:

David prayed to the Lord for healing, but he also admitted that he had sinned against God. Having a right relationship with God through confession and repentance of sin is the first step toward healing.

Another key to healing is having faith that God can and will heal you. When you pray, you must ask in faith. You must also accept that it is God who decides to show mercy. You can neither choose it nor work for it. If it is God's will and plan to heal you, then you will be healed—instantly and completely.

But the ultimate healing, available to anyone who believes, happens when you accept Jesus Christ as your Savior and Lord. When God forgives your sins, your dead spirit is raised to life, and you are brought into God's presence forever. "Praise the Lord, the God of Israel, who lives from everlasting to everlasting. Amen and amen!" (verse 13)

PSALM 42

Verse 11: "Why am I discouraged? Why is my heart so sad? I will put my hope in God! I will praise him again—my Savior and my God!"

Reflection:

When your heart is breaking, you may long for God and ask him, "When can I go and be with you?"

When you have tears for food day and night, you may remember the good old days and how things used to be.

When you are discouraged, you may say, "Why is my heart so sad?"

When you are experiencing grief, you may question God, "Why have you forgotten me?"

God understands that we will have times of sadness, grief, and discouragement. So how should we, born-again Christians, respond? By putting our hope in Jesus, our Savior. By remembering how God has poured his unfailing love upon us. By singing praises and giving thanks to the Lord. And by praying to God who has given us life.

PSALM 43

Verse 4: "There I will go to the altar of God, to God—the source of all my joy. I will praise you with my harp, O God, my God!"

Reflection:

Happiness is feeling good because your circumstances are good. It is determined by what happens to you. Joy is inner stability and tranquility from Christ, regardless of external circumstances. It comes from a relationship with God through his Son, Jesus. Joy that is Christ-based is not affected by circumstances. Since no one can take your Jesus, no one can take your joy.

Are you letting the light and truth of God's Word guide the way that you live? Do you praise and magnify God rather than worry and magnify your problems? Is Jesus the source of all your joy?

PSALM 44

Verses 13-14: "You let our neighbors mock us. We are an object of scorn and derision to those around us. You have made us the butt of their jokes; they shake their heads at us in scorn."

Reflection:

When people are angry at God, they will take it out on the godly people around them. This has been proven to be true through the ages as followers of Jesus are killed every day—slaughtered like sheep—for the sake of Christ. Christians are humiliated, taunted, and joked about. Believers are hated, mocked, scorned, and butchered. Doesn't this sound familiar? Doesn't it make sense that if Satan did these things to Jesus, he would also do it to Jesus' followers?

Even though the enemy is strong, Jesus Christ is stronger. Only by his power can we push back our foes. Only in his name can we have victory over the enemies of sin, fear, and death. Only by trusting in him can we have peace. And only by faith in him can we have salvation and eternal life.

PSALM 45

Verses 6-7a: "Your throne, O God, endures forever and ever. You rule with a scepter of justice. You love justice and hate evil."

Reflection:

God always judges fairly. So, may we, his children, not retaliate when we are insulted or threaten revenge when we suffer. Instead, may we listen and take to heart God's promises in the Bible. And may we leave our case in the hands of our heavenly Father.

May we bring honor to the name of Jesus Christ by not paying back evil with evil but by conquering evil with good. May we patiently wait for the Most High to act on our behalf. And may we believe that, in his justice, our glorious King will ride out to victory, defending the truth and paying back those who persecute us.

Read

PSALM 46

Verse 7:   "The Lord of Heavens Armies is here among us; the God of Israel is our fortress."

Reflection:

When the culture is in chaos and the world is in an uproar, it's easy to get caught up in the trouble around us. But when we do, it only makes us fearful, weak, anxious, and vulnerable.

The Lord of Heaven Armies—Jesus Christ—is here among us. He is always ready to help those who belong to him. Jesus is our refuge and strength, so we have no reason to fear in times of trouble.

The God of Israel is our fortress and our protector—today and forever. So be still and know that he is God.

PSALM 47

Verse 2:   "For the Lord Most High is awesome.
                He is the great King of all the earth."

Reflection:

Do you ever feel like the world is out of control? It's not—here's why:

> ➤ Jesus Christ, God the Son, is King over all the earth.

> ➤ Jesus Christ, who reigns above the nations, ascended to heaven after he rose from the grave.

> ➤ Jesus Christ, who controls all the kings of the earth, is on his throne at the right hand of God the Father.

> ➤ Jesus Christ, the Lord Most High, rules over everything, and he is in complete control.

> ➤ Jesus Christ, the great King of all the earth, deserves our joyful praise and honor as he will put the enemies of the people he loves beneath their feet.

> ➤ Jesus Christ is awesome!

PSALM 48

Verses 1-3: "How great is the Lord, how deserving of praise, in the city of our God, which sits on his holy mountain! It is high and magnificent; the whole earth rejoices to see it! Mount Zion, the holy mountain, is the city of the great King! God himself is in Jerusalem's towers, revealing himself as its defender."

Reflection:

After the final judgment, there will be a new heaven and a new earth. The new Jerusalem—the holy city—will be the place of God's throne. He will live among his people whose names are written in the Lambs Book of Life. God will illuminate the city with his glory. There will be no evil, no tears, no death, and no pain.

One day, believers will see the glorious city of the Lord of Heaven's Armies that is written about in the Bible. We will walk around the city of our God and be stunned by its marvelous beauty. But while we are still living here on the old earth, we can rejoice that our names are written in heaven and trust in this promise: "He is our God forever, and he will guide us until we die." (verse 14b)

PSALM 49

Verse 1:   "Listen to this, all you people! Pay attention, everyone in the world!"

Reflection:

Those who listen to God's wisdom and pay attention to his Word should not fear when trouble or death comes because God will redeem the life of those who trust in the Lord Jesus as their Savior. They will be snatched from the power of the grave and instantly be in heaven when they take their last breath!

Those who are rich—and without the Lord Jesus—trust in their wealth. They can never pay God enough money to live forever or buy their way out of death. Their riches will not be taken with them to the grave. Their grand estates on earth will not translate into heavenly estates. Those who boast of their wealth may be applauded for their success in this life, but their fame will not last. Eventually, they will die, just like animals. This is the fate of fools.

PSALM 50

Verse 1: "The Lord, the Mighty One, is God, and he has spoken; he has summoned all humanity from where the sun rises to where it sets."

Reflection:

God wants thankfulness, not burnt offerings or animal sacrifices, from his people. Giving thanks is a sacrifice that truly honors God. All the world and everything in it belongs to God, so everything we have is from him—the sun, the plants, the animals, our life. We have so much to be thankful for.

May we offer God, through Jesus, a continual sacrifice of praise. May we be his faithful people who give him thanks and keep to his path. May we call on God when we are in trouble and trust that he will rescue us. And then, may we give him thanks and glory once again!

PSALM 51

Verses 1-2: "Have mercy on me, O God, because of your unfailing love. Because of your great compassion, blot out the stain of my sins. Wash me clean from my guilt. Purify me from my sin."

Reflection:

King David, who was once so close with the Lord, had sinned by committing adultery with Bathsheba and shedding the blood of her husband. David was haunted by his sins day and night. He felt distant from God, separated from his presence, guilty, and broken.

Like David, we are all born with fallen, human, sinful natures, and we need to repent regularly for our sins and be forgiven. Because all sin is rebellion against God, only God can wash away the stain of sin with the blood of Jesus Christ. Only God, through his Son, can purify us from the guilt of sin and replace it with the joy of his salvation.

PSALM 52

Verse 1: "Why do you boast about your crimes, great warrior? Don't you realize that God's justice continues forever?"

Reflection:

God sees, hears, and knows everything. He knows the people who are great in their own eyes. He hears the boastful lies of those who love evil more than good. The Lord knows which people trust in their wealth instead of God. He sees them grow more and more bold in their wickedness. And he hears when they cut down others with their words. But in his justice, God will cut them down—once and for all!

"The righteous will see it and be amazed. They will laugh and say, 'Look at what happens to mighty warriors who do not trust in God.'" (verses 6-7a)

PSALM 53

Verse 1:   "Only fools say in their hearts, 'There is no God.' They are corrupt, and their actions are evil; not one of them does good!"

Reflection:

Because of our sinful nature, all people have turned away from God. But because of God's grace, he seeks us and rescues us by offering salvation through Jesus Christ. People who say there is no God are called fools by God. People who reject God are rejected by God. And when terror like they have never known before grips them, they will regret choosing evil over good, lies over truth, and Satan over Christ.

PSALM 54

Verse 1: "Come with great power, O God, and rescue me! Defend me with your might."

Reflection:

We may not be on the run like David was when he said this, but most people can identify with the desire to be rescued by God. When God's children pray to him in Jesus' name, he listens. He pays attention to our plea. He helps us triumph over our troubles.

May we remember that the Lord is our helper who gives us life and keeps us alive. May we recall that God will do what he promises in his Word. May our Savior turn the evil plans of our enemies against them. And may we praise God's name, for he is good!

PSALM 55

Verse 6-7: "Oh, that I had wings like a dove; then I would fly away and rest! I would fly far away to the quiet of the wilderness."

Reflection:

Have you ever wanted to get away from it all? Have you ever felt overwhelmed by your troubles, your enemies, your friends who betray you, or your fear? God tells us what to do. "Give your burdens to the Lord, and he will take care of you. He will not permit the godly to slip and fall." (verse 22) Jesus also said, "Come to me, all of you who are weary and carry heavy burdens, and I will give you rest." (Matthew 11:28)

So fly to Jesus in prayer—morning, noon, and night. Call on God for help. Give the Lord your troubles and burdens. Then rest.

PSALM 56

Verse 9b: "This I know: God is on my side."

Reflection:

God is on my side.

"I trust in God, so why should I be afraid? What can mere mortals do to me?" (verse 11)

God is on my side.

He cares about my sorrows, collects all my tears in his bottle, and records each one in his book.

God is on my side.

He has mercy on me. When I call him, he answers me, and I thank him for his help.

God is on my side.

He has rescued me from spiritual death. And he keeps my feet from slipping as I walk in his presence, in his life-giving light.

PSALM 57

Verses 7,9-10: "My heart is confident in you, O God; my heart is confident. No wonder I can sing your praises! I will thank you, Lord, among all the people. I will sing your praises among the nations. For your unfailing love is as high as the heavens. Your faithfulness reaches to the clouds."

Reflection:

Because of our heavenly Father's unfailing love and faithfulness, we can be confident in him. We can be confident in his protection. We can be confident that he will fulfill his purpose for us. We can be confident that he will send help from heaven. And we can be confident that he will rescue us. Because of our heavenly Father's unfailing love and faithfulness, through Jesus Christ our Lord, may we thank him and sing his praises every day.

PSALM 58

Verses 1-2: "Justice—do you rulers know the meaning of the word? Do you judge the people fairly? No! You plot injustice in your heart. You spread violence throughout the land."

Reflection:

We live in a world full of injustice—where right is called wrong and bad is called good. Where the godly are persecuted and the ungodly are celebrated. But God is not blind. In his justice, he will pay back those who persecute his children. Even if the leaders and judges of the world do not judge justly, God does. And he will reward those who live for him and bless those who hunger and thirst for justice.

"The godly will rejoice when they see injustice avenged. They will wash their feet in the blood of the wicked. Then, at last, everyone will say, 'There truly is a reward for those who live for God; surely there is a God who judges justly here on earth.'" (verses 10-11)

PSALM 59

Verse 17: "O my Strength, to you I sing praises, for you, O God, are my refuge, the God who shows me unfailing love."

Reflection:

The Bible tells us to fix our thoughts on what is true, honorable, right, pure, lovely, and admirable. We are to focus on things that are excellent and worthy of praise—like God and heaven.

Notice the dark tone of David's words when he focuses on his problems. "Rescue me from my enemies, O God. Protect me from those who have come to destroy me. Rescue me from these criminals; save me from these murderers. They have set an ambush for me. Fierce enemies are out there waiting, Lord, though I have not sinned or offended them." (verses 1-3)

Then, notice the confidence in David's words when he changes his focus, magnifying God instead of his problems. "But Lord, you laugh at them. You scoff at all the hostile nations. You are my strength; I wait for you to rescue me, for you, O God, are my fortress. In his unfailing love, my God will stand with me. He will let me look down in triumph on all my enemies." (verses 8-10)

May we learn to focus on our heavenly Father, the Lord Jesus Christ, and the indwelling Holy Spirit—not ourselves, others, or our situations. Each morning, may we sing with joy about God's unfailing love and unmatched power. And each night, may we rest in the safety of his presence.

PSALM 60

Verse 12a: "With God's help we will do mighty things..."

Reflection:

Before we were ever conceived, God knew us and had plans for our entire lives. We were created on purpose and for a purpose. We may not know all the details, but God does. And he will fulfill his purpose for our life, one day at a time.

In the end, we will be able to look back and see how it was God—not humans—that helped us accomplish mighty things that we would never have imagined. It was God who broke us, rescued us, and led us to victory. So live each day with hope for a good future as you trust God to help you achieve his plans.

PSALM 61

Verses 2-4: "From the ends of the earth, I cry to you for help when my heart is overwhelmed. Lead me to the towering rock of safety, for you are my safe refuge, a fortress where my enemies cannot reach me. Let me live forever in your sanctuary, safe beneath the shelter of your wings!"

Reflection:

Safety and security are basic human needs that rank second only to bare necessities for survival like food, water, clothing, sleep, and shelter. When we accept Jesus Christ as our Savior, we are eternally safe because we are in him, and he is in us. Our all-powerful God will not let anyone snatch us away from Jesus. Our salvation cannot be undone.

One day, the Lord will deliver us from every evil attack. He will bring us safely into his heavenly Kingdom, which is an inheritance reserved for those who belong to Jesus. And we will live with God and sing his praises forever!

PSALM 62

Verse 5a: "Let all that I am wait quietly before God..."

Reflection:

Sometimes, our prayers are not answered as quickly as we would like, and we must wait for the Lord. We can wait restlessly and anxiously, or we can wait quietly.

To wait quietly, we must trust Jesus at all times. We need to remind ourselves that our hope, our security, and our victory are found in God alone, not in people—even powerful people—or wealth. As we wait quietly before God, we learn that he is our refuge, our rock, and our fortress where no enemy can reach us. We learn not to be shaken by people and circumstances. And we learn that God has the power to repay people according to what they have done. When we wait quietly before God, he speaks to our heart, and we grow stronger and closer to him as we experience his unfailing love.

PSALM 63

Verse 1:   "O God, you are my God; I earnestly search for you. My soul thirsts for you; my whole body longs for you in this parched and weary land where there is no water."

Reflection:

Like we need water to quench our thirst, we need God to quench our parched and thirsty souls. Soul water cannot be found in the world—only God, through Jesus Christ, can provide it.

Jesus will satisfy you more than anything—more than gourmet food, more than material things, and more than wealth. Because of his unfailing love, Jesus helps us every day and holds us securely in his strong hands. Like David in the wilderness of Judah, may we earnestly search for Jesus, long for Jesus, thirst for Jesus, praise Jesus, meditate on Jesus, sing to Jesus, and cling to Jesus. Then, one day, we will see our Lord in his heavenly sanctuary, and we will gaze upon his glory and power forever!

PSALM 64

Verse 3: "They sharpen their tongues like swords and aim their bitter words like arrows."

Reflection:

Whatever is in a person's heart is revealed in their words, so bitter people will speak bitter words. We should not be surprised when unbelievers attack Christians with their words but know that God himself will shoot them with his arrows and their own tongues will ruin them.

"Yes, the human heart and mind are cunning." (verse 6b) As God's children, may we be filled with the Holy Spirit. May we have the mind of Christ so that we think the pure thoughts that Jesus might think and speak the godly words that Jesus might speak. May we make a practice of reading the Bible every day. As a result, may our heart, mind, and words be purified and transformed.

PSALM 65

Verse 8: "Those who live at the ends of the earth stand in awe of your wonders. From where the sun rises to where it sets, you inspire shouts of joy."

Reflection:

God's mighty power formed the mountains and the oceans. He takes care of the earth, providing food and beauty for us to enjoy. God makes the hard pathways overflow with abundance. He quiets the raging oceans and pounding waves.

When we are overwhelmed by our sins, God forgives them all through Jesus Christ, our Savior, and the hope of everyone on earth. Our Father faithfully answers our prayers with awesome deeds. What joy on earth for those whom God chooses to bring near! What festivities are in heaven for those who will live in his holy Temple forever!

PSALM 66

Verses 18-20: "If I had not confessed the sin in my heart, the Lord would not have listened. But God did listen! He paid attention to my prayer. Praise God, who did not ignore my prayer or withdraw his unfailing love from me."

Reflection:

Sin separates us from holy God. The only prayer that he will hear from a sinner is their prayer for salvation and forgiveness through Jesus Christ. Once a person has accepted Jesus (by faith) and his pure blood, which was shed as the only payment for our sins, they become a child of God with full access to him through prayer.

For believers, daily walking with Jesus (by faith) and confession of sin keeps our fellowship with our Father as close as it can be. We will discover, like the psalmist, that our lives are in God's good hands. His hands that perform awesome miracles for his people. His hands that bring us through fire and flood to a place of great abundance and blessing!

PSALM 67

Verse 1: "May God be merciful and bless us. May his face smile with favor on us."

Reflection:

When people and nations of the world praise God, the earth will yield its harvests.

When people and nations of the world sing for joy because God governs and guides them, he will be merciful.

When people and nations of the world fear God and follow his ways, he will smile with favor on them.

And when the people of the whole world know and accept God's saving power—through faith in Jesus Christ—he will richly bless them.

PSALM 68

Verse 20: "Our God is a God who saves! The Sovereign Lord rescues us from death."

Reflection:

God is a God of love. He carries his children in his arms each day and provides a bountiful harvest for his needy people. He is a Father to the fatherless and a defender of widows. He places lonely people in families and sets prisoners free.

God is a God of power. The earth trembles before him, and the sky pours down rain. The Lord gives the word, and his will is done. He rides across the heavens, and his voice thunders from the sky. His majesty shines down, and his strength is mighty. He gives power and strength to his people.

God is a God of justice. Those who hate God and reject Jesus are his enemies. He will blow them away like smoke. He will melt the wicked like wax in a fire. And those who love their guilty ways will run for their lives and perish in the presence of God. But the godly will rejoice and be glad in God's presence, singing loud praises to him. God will bring down the enemy and give treasures to his children. The awesome Lord God will live among the godly in his sanctuary forever. Praise God!

PSALM 69

Verse 1: "Save me, O God, for the floodwaters are up to my neck."

Reflection:

Do you ever feel like you are up to your neck with troubles? Are you exhausted from crying for help? Are your eyes swollen from weeping? Are you suffering in pain? Is your heart broken?

Jesus understands. He experienced the pain and insults of others when he hung on the cross. And as prophesied in verse 21, "they offered me sour wine for my thirst."

When you humbly go to God in prayer and repent of your sins, he will answer you with his sure salvation. With his saving power, he will rescue you from the pit of death. With his mercy, he will redeem you and free you. With his unfailing love, he will take care of you and comfort you.

"The humble will see their God at work and be glad. Let all who seek God's help be encouraged. For the Lord hears the cries of the needy." (verses 32-33a)

PSALM 70

Verse 1,5b: "Please, God, rescue me! Come quickly, Lord, and help me. You are my helper and my savior; O Lord, do not delay."

Reflection:

Sometimes, we will have storms in life, and we want to be rescued right away. One day Jesus told his disciples to get into a boat to cross to the other side of the lake. Jesus settled down for a nap in the stern and then a fierce storm came. The boat was filling with water, and they were in real danger. So the disciples woke Jesus up and he rebuked the wind and waves—and suddenly the storm stopped—and it was perfectly calm!

Jesus cares deeply for you and he knows when the storms are coming in your life, so he gets into your boat in advance. Sooner or later, the waves will rock you but remember that Jesus is with you. His intent is not that you panic but that, because of your faith, you will experience his power and peace.

PSALM 71

Verse 6: "Yes, you have been with me from birth; from my mother's womb you have cared for me. No wonder I am always praising you!"

Reflection:

Even before God formed you, he knew you and had a plan for your life. From within your mother's womb, he called you by name. God also calls us to become his children by being born again. When we are born again spiritually, our new life lasts forever because it comes from God who is eternal.

From the moment we accept Jesus Christ (God the Son) as our Savior, the Holy Spirit (God the Spirit) lives within us and is always with us. Even when we are old and gray, we are never abandoned by God.

PSALM 72

Verse 17:   "May the king's name endure forever; may it continue as long as the sun shines. May all nations be blessed through him and bring him praise."

Reflection:

Jesus Christ is the King of kings who lives from everlasting to everlasting. He loves justice and righteousness, and he will judge all people fairly for their lives are precious to him.

When Jesus comes again to rule, all kings will bow before him, and all nations will serve him. When the King of kings reigns, God's people will thrive like grass in a field, the whole earth will flourish and be filled with his glory, and his magnificent name will be praised forever. Amen and Amen!

PSALM 73

Verses 16-17: "So I tried to understand why the wicked prosper. But what a difficult task it is! Then I went into your sanctuary, O God, and I finally understood the destiny of the wicked."

Reflection:

Those who wear pride like a necklace are on a slippery path that will send them sliding over a cliff to destruction. Fat cats who have everything their hearts could wish for will be completely swept away by terrors. God laughs at the silly ideas of those who boast against the heavens and strut about on the earth. "What does God know?" they ask. "Does the Most High even know what's happening?" (verse 11) But God knows! He knows the destiny of the wicked is destruction.

So even though you see the wicked enjoying a life of ease, don't envy them. Don't have a bitter heart about those who scoff at God and speak evil. And don't get all torn up inside about why the ungodly seem to prosper.

Keep your heart pure. Keep yourself innocent. Desire God above anything on earth. Because God is good to his children, and those who belong to him have a glorious destiny that will last forever!

PSALM 74

Verses 7-8: "They burned your sanctuary to the ground. They defiled the place that bears your name. Then they thought, 'Let's destroy everything!' So they burned down all the places where God was worshiped."

Reflection:

Foolish nations and people dishonor the name of the Lord Jesus Christ. They destroy the places where God is worshiped and defile the things that bear his name.

Foolish nations and people insult Jesus and his followers. They smash the crosses and burn the churches where God's redeemed go to worship. They censor Christians and forbid the Bible.

Foolish nations and people think they can destroy God by destroying the things of God. But God cannot be destroyed! He is eternal, and so are his children.

God will not overlook the sins of his enemies forever. Eventually, he will unleash his powerful fist and destroy them. And the moment foolish people pass from this life to the next, they will know what fools they really are!

PSALM 75

Verse 1a: "We thank you, O God! We give thanks because you are near."

Reflection:

When the earth quakes and the people live in turmoil, God is near.

When the wicked raise their fists in defiance at the heavens, God is near.

When the proud boast with arrogance, God is near.

When the planned time arrives and justice is served against the wicked, God is near.

When the foaming wine of judgment is poured out for the wicked to drink, God is near.

When the strength of the wicked is broken, God is near.

When the power of the godly increases, God is near.

When people everywhere tell of his wonderful deeds, God is near.

PSALM 76

Verse 11b: "Let everyone bring tribute to the Awesome One."

Reflection:

He breaks the fiery arrows of the enemy and the weapons of war. He stands up to judge those who do evil and makes our boldest enemies lay still. He rescues the oppressed of the earth, and the kings of the earth fear him. He uses human defiance as a weapon and breaks the pride of princes.

The Lord, our God, is glorious, majestic—and awesome! May we remember his faithfulness. May we fear his power. May we honor his name. And may we trust his heart.

PSALM 77

Verse 2: "When I was in deep trouble, I searched for the Lord. All night long I prayed, with hands lifted toward heaven, but my soul was not comforted."

Reflection:

When we need God's help, but he is quiet, it can seem like he has abandoned us. We might begin to doubt God's unfailing love and feel rejected by him. Or perhaps we might even feel like God has turned his hand against us and his promises have failed.

In times of doubt (which is one of Satan's spiritual weapons) may we recall the wonderful deeds that God has done. May we keep thinking about his grace and compassion. May we focus on the Lord Jesus, our Shepherd, who redeems his people and leads them along the best path. And when we can't see the path, may we remember that in his holy and omnipotent way, God makes pathways that no one even knows are there!

PSALM 78

Verse 7-8: "So each generation should set its hope anew on God, not forgetting his glorious miracles and obeying his commands. Then they will not be like their ancestors—stubborn, rebellious, and unfaithful, refusing to give their hearts to God."

Reflection:

God wants us to believe in Jesus and trust him to care for us. He wants us to remember his glorious miracles and obey his commands. God wants us to teach others about him. He wants us to give him our hearts, not lip service. God Most High wants us to know him, through faith in Jesus, as our Redeemer and Father. God wants us to experience his love, forgiveness, and mercy. And God wants us to worship him alone, trusting him to guide us safely through the wilderness.

PSALM 79

Verse 9a: "Help us, O God of our salvation!"

Reflection:

God saves the prisoners of sin
who are condemned to die because of it.
God saves those on the brink of despair
by compassionately meeting their needs.
God saves his people,
his special possession, who are mocked by those around
them.
God saves his servants,
who have spilled blood for Jesus, by giving them eternal
life.
God saves his children,
the sheep of his pasture, for the glory and honor of his
name.
God saves his godly ones,
who will praise his greatness and thank him forever and
ever.
God will save you
and forgive your sins when you call upon the name of
his Son, Jesus Christ, to be your Savior.

PSALM 80

Verse 19: "Turn us again to yourself, O Lord God of Heaven's Armies. Make your face shine down upon us. Only then will we be saved."

Reflection:

Why wasn't God's face shining down upon the Israelites? Because they had abandoned him.

When God's people abandon him, it can feel like he is distant. God may not respond to their prayers like he once did. In order to get their attention, God may turn against his disobedient children and discipline them like the loving Father that he is. But God will never abandon his true children. Instead, he wants them to abandon their shameful ways and turn back to him.

PSALM 81

Verses 11-12: "But no, my people wouldn't listen. Israel did not want me around. So I let them follow their own stubborn desires, living according to their own ideas."

Reflection:

Those who listen to God are the ones who truly love him. God doesn't force people to obey him, but the ones who do are blessed.

May God take the load from their shoulders and free them from heavy tasks. May he save them when they are in trouble and rescue them from impossible situations. May God subdue their enemies and free them from their foes. And may he feed them the finest foods and satisfy them with his love.

God doesn't make his children listen to him—many don't—but those who do will experience life at its best.

PSALM 82

Verse 2: "How long will you hand down unjust decisions by favoring the wicked?"

Reflection:

Sometimes, God's ways seem unjust. We don't understand why he allows certain things to happen as they do. God pronounces judgment on heavenly beings and on all the nations of the earth. But just as the heavens are higher than the earth, God's ways are higher than our ways, and God's thoughts are higher than our thoughts. We may not always understand God, but we can always trust him and know that, in the end, justice will prevail, righteousness will be upheld, and the children of the Most High will be eternally satisfied!

PSALM 83

Verse 4: "Come," they say, "let us wipe out Israel as a nation. We will destroy the very memory of its existence."

Reflection:

People said this at the time of Asaph, and people are still saying this today. The wicked, under the influence of Satan, will always conspire against the things that God created and loves—especially the nation of Israel and his precious people. These arrogant enemies of God, who devise schemes against his children, have not yet learned that Jesus Christ alone is Lord, supreme over all the earth. God is not blind or deaf to their evil ways. He will not be silent forever. And unless they submit to Jesus Christ as Savior, they will die in utter disgrace and be terrified for eternity.

PSALM 84

Verses 1-2: "How lovely is your dwelling place, O Lord of Heaven's Armies. I long, yes, I faint with longing to enter the courts of the Lord. With my whole being, body and soul, I will shout joyfully to the living God."

Reflection:

Thinking about heaven makes us long to be there. In our eternal home, the Lord will be our sun. We will sing praises to our King as we appear before him. In comparison, just one day in heaven will be better than a thousand days anywhere on earth!

When we walk through the Valley of Weeping, may we set our minds on the things above. May we come to realize that the Lord will withhold no good thing from those who do what is right. And may we continue to grow stronger as God gives us grace, favor, and blessings.

What joy awaits those who will live in God's house forever! What joy awaits those whose strength comes from the Lord! What joy awaits those who trust in Jesus Christ, the Lord of Heaven's Armies, as their Savior, their King, and their God!

PSALM 85

Verse 8: "I listen carefully to what God the Lord is saying, for he speaks peace to his faithful people. But let them not return to their foolish ways."

Reflection:

God forgives the guilt of people and covers all the sins of the world with the sacrificial blood of his Son, Jesus Christ. God grants his unfailing love and salvation to those who accept Jesus as their Savior.

God speaks truth and peace to his faithful people—at all times and in every situation. He shows his unfailing love to those who fear him. God's righteousness smiles down from heaven. And the Lord pours down his blessings on those who have received his gift of salvation.

PSALM 86

Verse 1a: "Bend down, O Lord, and hear my prayer."

Reflection:

Protect me, save me, be merciful to me, give me happiness, teach me your ways, and grant me purity of heart. Why would David think that God would answer these prayer requests? Because he was devoted to the Lord. He served, trusted, and gave himself to the Lord. David called upon the Lord in faith and lived according to God's truth.

God is so good and merciful. May he forgive your sins and answer your prayers too—when you give yourself to him.

God is filled with unfailing love and faithfulness. Like David, whenever you are in trouble and need his help, may the Lord bend down and hear your urgent cry.

God's love for you is very great. May those who belong to Jesus be rescued from the depths of death and receive God's favor, comfort, and strength.

PSALM 87

Verse 87: "On the holy mountain stands the city founded by the Lord. He loves the city of Jerusalem more than any other city in Israel. O city of God, what glorious things are said of you!"

Reflection:

One day, the holy city of new Jerusalem will come down out of heaven like a bride beautifully dressed for her husband. This will be the eternal city of God, the city personally blessed by him, where all who have received eternal life will be citizens.

New Jerusalem will be a glorious place full of love, joy, and peace where the Most High God will live with the true children of Abraham, who belong to Christ. People from every tribe, language, and nation will play music and sing as they worship the Lord—the source of their life.

PSALM 88

Verse 18b: "Darkness is my closest friend."

Reflection:

When sickness and troubles weigh us down, it is hard to have a positive outlook on life. When our strength and our friends are gone, we can feel forgotten by God. And when we feel helpless and desperate for relief, it's like God is angry and has thrown us into the lowest pit.

God is good and does no wrong. We don't always understand why we suffer, but God does. Sometimes, he gets our attention through adversity, and he rescues those who suffer by means of their suffering. But as God's children, we can rest assured that he is always with us, his grace is sufficient, and his strength is made perfect in our weakness.

PSALM 89

Verse 8: "O Lord God of Heavens Armies! Where is there anyone as mighty as you, O Lord? You are entirely faithful."

Reflection:

God is so awesome that even the highest angelic powers stand in awe of him. The mightiest angel cannot compare with the Lord. "He is far more awesome than all who surround his throne." (verse 7b) The heavens, the earth, and everything in the world is God's—he created it all with his glorious strength.

God is holy and he cannot lie. Truth, unfailing love, justice, righteousness, and faithfulness are the foundation of his throne. God will never stop loving his children or fail to keep his promises. Happy are those who can call him Father, God, and the Rock of my salvation, for they will walk in the light of his presence and praise the Lord forever. Amen!

PSALM 90

Verse 2: "Before the mountains were born, before you gave birth to the earth and the world, from beginning to end, you are God."

Reflection:

You are God, and for you, a thousand years is as brief as one day.

You are God, who sees all our secret sins.

You are God, who turns people back to dust.

You are God, whose wrath is as awesome as the fear you deserve.

You are God, who teaches us so that we may grow in wisdom.

You are God, who satisfies us each morning with your unfailing love.

You are God, who gives us gladness in proportion to our former misery.

You are God, who replaces the evil years with good.

You are God, who shows us your approval and makes our efforts successful.

PSALM 91

Verse 1a: "Those who live in the shelter of the Most High…"

Reflection:

The Most High God promises that we, his children, who live in his shelter:

➢ Will find rest because we trust in God.

➢ Are covered, sheltered, and rescued by the Almighty.

➢ Wear God's faithful promises as our armor and protection.

➢ Have no reason to fear—by day or night.

➢ Will not be conquered by evil but will trample and crush it.

➢ Are protected by God's angels wherever we go.

➢ Can call on the Lord Jesus for help, and he will answer.

➢ Live forever in the presence of the Lord, who we love.

➢ Have eternal life and salvation through Jesus Christ.

PSALM 92

Verses 1-2: "It is good to give thanks to the Lord, to sing praises to the Most High. It is good to proclaim your unfailing love in the morning, your faithfulness in the evening,"

Reflection:

As we start our day in prayer, may we thank the Lord for his unfailing love.

As we walk through our day in prayer, may we thank God for being just and holy. May we thank him for making us strong. May we thank him for our salvation and his indwelling Holy Spirit. And may we thank him for transplanting us from Satan's house of downfall, defeat, and destruction to God's house of favor, fruitfulness, and flourishing.

And as we end our day in prayer, may we be thrilled to recall all the Lord has done for us that day and thank him for his faithfulness.

PSALM 93

Verse 1a: "The Lord is King!"

Reflection:

From the everlasting past—before the beginning of time—the throne of God has stood. "Indeed, the Lord is robed in majesty and armed with strength." (verse 1b)

Holy, holy, holy is the Lord God Almighty who was, and is, and is to come. He is mightier than the raging seas. He is more powerful than the pounding waves. And he is stronger than the roaring thunder. The royal laws of the Lord cannot be changed.

The Lord Jesus Christ is the Alpha and Omega, the First and the Last, the Beginning and the End. His holy reign is from eternity past to eternity future, forever and ever. Amen!

PSALM 94

Verse 1: "O Lord, the God of vengeance, O God of vengeance, let your glorious justice shine forth!"

Reflection:

Evil people crush God's people, hurting those who are followers of Jesus. They think God isn't looking or he doesn't care.

Think again, you fools! When will you ever learn? Do you think God, the one who made your ears, is deaf? Do you think God, the one who made your eyes, is blind? God knows everything, including what you are thinking and doing.

The Lord will not abandon his children, his special possession. The Judge of the earth will give the wicked what they deserve. He will turn the sins of evil people back on them. The Lord our God will destroy them.

PSALM 95

Verses 6-7a: "Come, let us worship and bow down. Let us kneel before the Lord our maker, for he is our God."

Reflection:

The Lord is a great God! He created the earth and everything in it—the mighty mountains, the land, the sea, the people—and he holds it all in his hands.

The Lord is the Rock of our salvation! Jesus is our Shepherd, and we are the people he watches over, the sheep under his care. May we sing and shout with joy, praise, and thankfulness.

The Lord is a great King! May we listen to his voice today and do what he tells us. May we not test God's patience or harden our hearts and turn away from Jesus. Because if you do, you may never enter God's place of rest.

PSALM 96

Verses 4-5: "Great is the Lord! He is most worthy of praise! He is to be feared above all gods. The gods of other nations are mere idols, but the Lord made the heavens!"

Reflection:

All religions, except Christianity, are man-made and require some type of work to earn your way to heaven. But Jesus Christ did all the work needed for you to go to heaven. He shed his blood and died on the cross as the perfect sacrifice for our sins. Jesus was without sin, but because of his love for us, he willingly took the punishment for the sins of the world. So when we repent of our sins and put our faith and trust in Jesus as our Savior and Lord, we are forgiven and saved eternally. This is the Good News that Jesus saves!

The Bible tells us that Jesus is coming again. He is coming to judge the earth. He will judge the people fairly, the world with justice, and the nations with truth. And for those who belong to Jesus, you will be judged "not guilty."

PSALM 97

Verses 11-12: "Light shines on the godly, and joy on those whose hearts are right. May all who are godly rejoice in the Lord and praise his holy name!"

Reflection:

The Lord Jesus Christ is supreme over all the earth, and he is exalted far above all gods. The heavens proclaim his righteousness, dark clouds surround him, fire spreads ahead of him, his lightning flashes across the world, and the mountains melt like wax before him.

One day, Jesus will return, and his godly people will be overjoyed! They will finally be forever rescued from the power of the wicked. But those who worship idols and brag about their worthless gods will be disgraced, for every god must bow to King Jesus.

PSALM 98

Verses 1-2: "Sing a new song to the Lord, for he has done wonderful deeds. His right hand has won a mighty victory; his holy arm has shown his saving power! The Lord has announced his victory and has revealed his righteousness to every nation!"

Reflection:

It is so good to know that as children of God, we are on the winning team. In Christ, we are victorious! And we already know how history (his.story) ends.

Bible prophecy was written so that so we can know what the future holds and be prepared. It also gives us hope and assurance that the best is yet to come. Jesus is coming again. What a victory celebration we will have with our Lord and King, praising him and singing for joy!

PSALM 99

Verse 4: "Mighty King, lover of justice, you have established fairness. You have acted with justice and righteousness throughout Israel."

Reflection:

The Lord is King! He sits in majesty on his throne with cherubim on each side. His name is great and awesome. And he is exalted above all nations.

The Lord our God loves justice and acts with righteousness. He is a forgiving God, but he also punishes us when we do wrong. The Lord answers those who call to him for help. He speaks to us and gives us his Word so that we may know him and follow him.

"Exalt the Lord our God, and worship at his holy mountain in Jerusalem, for the Lord our God is holy! (verse 9)

Read

PSALM 100

Verse 4: "Enter his gates with thanksgiving; go into his courts with praise. Give thanks to him and praise his name."

Reflection:

➤ As humans

may we be thankful that God made us and gave us physical life.

➤ As God's people

may we be thankful that he has given us spiritual life and victory over sin and death through our Lord Jesus Christ.

➤ As children of God

may we be thankful that we are his. He surrounds us continuously and welcomes us into his presence.

➤ And as the sheep of his pasture

may we give thanks to the Lord for his unfailing love, faithfulness, and goodness. May we worship him and praise him for leading us, protecting us and taking care of us.

PSALM 101

Verse 1: "I will sing of your love and justice, Lord. I will praise you with songs."

Reflection:

David pledged to live a life that was honoring to the Lord. As Christians, if we follow his example, we, too, will please Jesus with our conduct. May we:

- Be careful to live a blameless life.
- Lead a life of integrity.
- Refuse to look at anything vile or vulgar.
- Have nothing to do with people who deal crookedly.
- Reject perverse ideas.
- Stay away from every evil.
- Not tolerate slanderers, liars, and deceivers.
- Not endure wicked, conceited, and prideful people.
- Look for people of faith, who are above reproach, to be our friends.

PSALM 102

Verses 11-12: "My life passes as swiftly as the evening shadows. I am withering away like grass.

But you, O Lord, will sit on your throne forever. Your fame will endure to every generation."

Reflection:

Have you ever been overwhelmed with trouble? This is the prayer of one who is pouring out his problems to the Lord. Notice that in the first eleven verses, the psalmist is focusing on himself, and the tone is dark and hopeless. But in verse twelve, he shifts his focus to God, and there is a sense of hope for the future. This is an example for us. When we resolutely put our hope in God and focus on him rather than our circumstances, we are demonstrating faith.

God is always the same. He is always faithful, and he will always sit on his throne. His children will eternally live in security and thrive in his presence. God is worthy of our trust in times of distress—and always.

PSALM 103

Verse 1: "Let all that I am praise the Lord; with my whole heart, I will praise his holy name."

Reflection:

God is so compassionate and merciful. He knows how weak we are and that our time on earth is short. Like a flower, we bloom and die.

If it wasn't for God's love, we would be punished eternally for our sins—as we deserve. But Jesus came down from heaven, and his blood paid the penalty for all our sins. When we accept Jesus as our Savior and Lord, we are forgiven and redeemed from death. God removes our sins as far from us as the east is from the west.

As God's children, we are blessed by his unfailing love that is as great as the height of the heavens above the earth. We are crowned by our Father with tender mercies, and our life is filled with good things. To all who are treated unfairly, the Lord gives righteousness and justice. And from his heavenly throne, God Almighty sends angels who serve him to carry out his will and plans concerning us, his beloved children.

"Let all that I am praise the Lord; may I never forget the good things he does for me." (verse 2)

PSALM 104

Verse 1a: "Let all that I am praise the Lord. O Lord my God, how great you are!"

Reflection:

God is dressed in a robe of light, honor, and majesty. In wisdom, he made the earth and all its creatures. The Lord takes pleasure in all that he has made, and every living thing depends on him. When God opens his hand to feed the animals, they are richly satisfied. When he gives them his breath, life is created. And when he takes away their breath, they die and turn to dust.

May all my thoughts be pleasing to the Lord. May I sing to my Creator as long as I live. And may I praise the Lord my God to my last breath. Praise the Lord!

PSALM 105

Verse 19:   "Until the time came to fulfill his dreams, the Lord tested Joseph's character."

Reflection:

When Joseph was young, God gave him a dream that one day, his family would bow low before him. When he shared it with his brothers, they hated him. When he shared it with his father, Jacob, he scolded him. Joseph was sold as a slave by his brothers and was later put in prison. Eventually, Pharaoh sent for him, set him free, and put Joseph in charge of his household, possessions, and the food supply in Egypt.

When we endure difficult times, may we—like Joseph—stay true to the Lord. When our faith is tested, may we continually search for the Lord and for his strength. And may we remember that God is in control of everything that happens, and he intends it all for good.

PSALM 106

Verse 1: "Praise the Lord! Give thanks to the Lord, for he is good! His faithful love endures forever."

Reflection:

God's love truly is unfailing. Even after the Israelites continually forgot his many acts of kindness to them, he remembered his covenant with them. God's chosen people tested his patience and refused to believe his promise to care for them. Instead, they grumbled and refused to obey the Lord. Over and over, God's special possession rebelled against him and defiled themselves. Again and again, he rescued them, but they were finally destroyed by their sin.

Like the Israelites, we have sinned. We have done wrong. We have acted wickedly. So may we call upon the Lord Jesus, because of his unfailing love, to forgive us, save us, and rescue us. And may the Lord show favor to his people who do what is right.

PSALM 107

Verse 6: "Lord, help! they cried in their trouble, and he rescued them from their distress."

Reflection:

When people cry out to the Lord for help, he saves them. He leads the lost to safety. He satisfies the thirst of the wanderer. And he fills the hunger of those who are near spiritual death.

The Most High breaks those who rebel against his Word, but he also snaps the chains of people imprisoned in darkness and gloom. By his power, God speaks, and people are healed—snatched from death's door. The Lord calms the storms to a whisper and stills the waves. God blesses the godly with families, fruitfulness, and bumper crops.

Praise the Lord for his great love and the wonderful things he has done!

PSALM 108

Verses 4-5: "For your unfailing love is higher than the heavens. Your faithfulness reaches to the clouds. Be exalted, O God, above the highest heavens. May your glory shine over all the earth."

Reflection:

As believers in Jesus Christ, may we have confidence in God's unfailing love and faithfulness.

As children of God, may we depend on our Father and know that he will answer us, and by his power, he will save us.

And as his beloved people, may we trust the promises of God and realize that he will help us do mighty things!

PSALM 109

Verse 28: "Then let them curse me if they like, but you will bless me! When they attack me, they will be disgraced! But I, your servant, will go right on rejoicing!"

Reflection:

When the wicked slander and tell lies about the godly, may we pray for them. When they surround us with hateful words and fight against us for no reason, may we forgive them. When evil people curse God and others, may we bless them. And when they repay evil for good, may we give them love for hatred.

Be assured, God blesses you when people mock, persecute, lie, and say all sorts of evil things against you because you are a follower of Jesus. And in his justice, God himself will pay back the wicked.

PSALM 110

Verse 3b: "You are arrayed in holy garments, and your strength will be renewed each day like the morning dew."

Reflection:

Like the Lord Jesus, who is referred to in this Psalm, his followers are holy in God's eyes. Also, like the Lord Jesus, who is a priest forever in the order of Melchizedek, we are made priests of God through Christ. The Lord Jesus sits in the place of honor at God's right hand, and because we are united with Christ, we are also seated with him in the heavenly realms. One day, like the Lord Jesus, we will receive our eternal bodies that never grow weak or old. But until that day comes, God will protect his children and renew our strength each day like the morning dew.

PSALM 111

Verse 2: "How amazing are the deeds of the Lord! All who delight in him should ponder them."

Reflection:

As we think about God's wonderful works and his amazing grace and mercy, may we ponder the most loving thing that he did—pay a full ransom for his people with the blood of Jesus Christ. What must it have been like for our heavenly Father to send Jesus, his beloved Son, to earth? Jesus left heaven and came down to earth for one reason alone—love.

Because of Jesus's sacrificial and awe-inspiring love, he came to this earth to be born in a manger, live a sinless life, and die on the cross for the sins of the world. God guarantees his covenant of eternal life through faith in Jesus. Everything he does is just and good and reveals his glory and majesty. Praise the Lord forever!

PSALM 112

Verse 1: "Praise the Lord! How joyful are those who fear the Lord and delight in obeying his commands."

Reflection:

People who fear God and delight in obeying his Word:

➤ Are generous, compassionate, and righteous.

➤ Do not fear bad news.

➤ Are confident and fearless because they trust in the Lord to take care of them.

➤ Will not be overcome by evil.

➤ Wait to see their enemies defeated.

➤ Will have influence, honor, and wealth.

➤ Have light in the darkness.

➤ Will be long remembered, and their good deeds will last forever.

PSALM 113

Verses 1-2: "Praise the Lord! Yes, give praise, O servants of the Lord. Praise the name of the Lord! Blessed be the name of the Lord now and forever."

Reflection:

May we praise the Lord because he is above all—so high above that he must stoop down to look on heaven and earth.

May we praise the Lord for creating all things and for giving us life.

May we praise the Lord for choosing us to be adopted into his family by bringing us to himself through Jesus Christ.

May we praise the Lord for changing our eternal address from hell to heaven.

May we praise the Lord for his love, grace, and mercy.

May we praise the Lord our God, who is enthroned on high, because no one can compare to him!

PSALM 114

Verse 7: "Tremble, O earth, at the presence of the Lord, at the presence of the God of Jacob."

Reflection:

Our God, the maker of heaven and earth, can do anything. When the Israelites escaped from Egypt, they faced oversized obstacles and had numerous needs on their journey to the Promised Land. So, God's people had to trust him to take care of them—and he did.

If God can divide the waters of the Red Sea and the Jordan River for the Israelites, don't you think he can also move obstacles in your life? If God can make a spring of water flow from solid rock for the family of Jacob, is there any doubt that he can and will provide for you? The struggles in life are real, but so is the help of God.

PSALM 115

Verse 1: "Not to us, O Lord, not to us, but to your name goes all the glory for your unfailing love and faithfulness."

Reflection:

Our God, who made heaven and earth, is not like an idol made by human hands. Idols cannot speak, see, or hear. They are just powerless objects. But our omnipotent God is in the heavens, and he does as he wishes.

Our God is our helper and our shield. May those who belong to Jesus trust him to help them in all things and surround them with his shield of love.

Our God remembers us and richly blesses those who fear him. May we praise the Lord our God, both now and forever!

PSALM 116

Verses 12,17:   "What can I offer the Lord for all he has done for me? I will offer you a sacrifice of thanksgiving and call on the name of the Lord."

Reflection:

Thank you, Lord, for hearing my voice.

Thank you, Lord, for bending down to listen to my prayers.

Thank you, Lord, for being good, kind, and merciful.

Thank you, Lord, for protecting those with childlike faith.

Thank you, Lord, for saving me from death.

Thank you, Lord, for your presence with me here on earth.

Thank you, Lord, for freeing me from my chains.

Thank you, Lord, for caring deeply when your precious ones die.

PSALM 117

Verse 2: "For his unfailing love for us is powerful; the Lord's faithfulness endures forever."

Reflection:

Because of his unfailing love, the Word—the Father's one and only Son, also known as Jesus Christ—became human and made his home among us. Because of his unfailing love, God presented Jesus as the sacrifice for sin, freeing us from the penalty of our sins when we believe in Jesus. And because of his unfailing love, God made a way for the entire world—who is guilty before him—to be declared not guilty through faith in Jesus.

Because of his faithfulness, the prophesied Messiah has come, and the Bible does not end at Malachi. Because of his faithfulness, we celebrate Christmas. Because of his faithfulness, we have the gospel, the promise of hope, and salvation. And because of his faithfulness, we have the comfort of knowing that one day we will have a glorious resurrection and a mansion in heaven.

PSALM 118

Verses 5-8: "In my distress I prayed to the Lord, and the Lord answered me and set me free. The Lord is for me, so I will have no fear. What can mere people do to me? Yes, the Lord is for me; he will help me. I will look in triumph at those who hate me. It is better to take refuge in the Lord than to trust in people."

Reflection:

Jesus is the Stone that the builders rejected, and now he has become the most important Stone. Without the Lord Jesus Christ as your Savior, you cannot claim these truths as your own.

The Lord is God. May he shine upon you and help you. When enemies attack, may the Lord Jesus rescue you and give you success. May he answer your prayers and give you songs of victory so you can tell others what the Lord has done. Bless the Lord; his faithful love endures forever!

PSALM 119 (ALEPH)

Verses 1-2: "Joyful are people of integrity, who follow the instructions of the Lord. Joyful are those who obey his laws and search for him with all their hearts."

Reflection:

How does your life compare with God's Word? Are you ashamed to say, or are you joyful?

- ➤ When our actions are consistent with God's commands, we have nothing to be ashamed of.
- ➤ When we learn God's righteous regulations and live in obedience, we show him true thanks.
- ➤ And when we walk in the paths of the Lord and do not compromise with evil, we will be joyful.

PSALM 119 (BETH)

Verse 9a: "How can a young person stay pure?"

Reflection:

There are 9 things we can do at any age to help us stay pure and not sin against God:

1. Obey God's commands.
2. Memorize God's Word.
3. Listen to and learn from godly teachers.
4. Praise the Lord.
5. Read the Bible.
6. Study Scripture.
7. Delight in the Lord's decrees.
8. Reflect on God's ways.
9. Remember God's Word.

PSALM 119 (GIMEL)

Verse 18: "Open my eyes to see the wonderful truths in your instructions."

Reflection:

When we, followers of Jesus, read the Bible, the indwelling Holy Spirit teaches us. He opens our minds and helps us understand the wonderful truths of Scripture. He opens our eyes and helps us to see how we can obey God's Word and apply it to our daily lives.

When we are troubled, meditating on Scripture refocuses our mind on God's truth and wisdom. So, rather than letting the twisted truth of this cursed world (where we live as foreigners) influence our thinking, may we fill our minds with the good things of God that are true, pure, wise, excellent, and worthy of praise.

PSALM 119 (DALETH)

Verse 27: "Help me understand the meaning of your commandments, and I will meditate on your wonderful deeds."

Reflection:

It is a privilege to know what God says—it keeps us from lying to ourselves and helps us to live obediently and faithfully for Jesus.

Before reading the Bible, pray and ask God to open your eyes and reveal the truth. Then, as you read and meditate on Scripture, the Holy Spirit will speak to your heart, teach you, and expand your understanding. You will be revived and encouraged as God's speaks to you through his Word, which is truth.

PSALM 119 (HE)

Verse 35: "Make me walk along the path of your commands, for that is where my happiness is found."

Reflection:

Nothing this world has to offer will satisfy a person who is created to know God. True happiness is found by having a relationship with God through his Son, Jesus Christ, and walking in his path. The Lord Jesus will renew our life with his goodness and help us to abandon our shameful ways when we love him with all our hearts and keep his instructions.

Eagerly obeying God rather than loving money and turning to his Word rather than to worthless things brings life-giving satisfaction.

PSALM 119 (WAW)

Verse 43: "Do not snatch your word of truth from me, for your regulations are my only hope."

Reflection:

May we devote ourselves to the commandments of the Lord and walk in freedom.

May we speak to others about God's laws and not be ashamed.

May we delight in the Lord's decrees because we love them.

May we meditate on our Father's unfailing love and his promised salvation.

May we trust in God's Word and keep his instructions forever and ever.

PSALM 119 (ZAYIN)

Verse 50: "Your promise revives me; it comforts me in all my troubles."

Reflection:

In difficult times, may we be rooted in God's truth and revived by his promises.

➤ Meditating on the Word of God brings comfort.

➤ Remembering the promises of the Bible gives us hope.

➤ Focusing on the truth of God can make negative emotions disappear.

➤ Reflecting on who the Lord is causes people to want to obey him.

➤ Rejecting Jesus Christ and his instructions results in wickedness.

➤ Obeying God's commandments is the best way to spend your life.

PSALM 119 (HETH)

Verse 59: "I pondered the direction of my life, and I turned to follow your laws."

Reflection:

Have you ever stopped to think about the direction of your life? God, your Creator, knows the purpose and plan for your life—but unless you know God, you won't know his plan.

When we turn away from sin and turn to follow Jesus, we become a child of God, and Jesus becomes our Savior, Lord, Friend, and Brother. The Bible says that Jesus is also the Vine that we, as branches, get our life from. When we stay connected to and dependent on him, we will produce the fruit that we were created to bear. But without Jesus, we can do nothing.

PSALM 119
(TETH)

Verse 68a: "You are good and do only good."

Reflection:

God is good, and he does only good. There are times when our heavenly Father, like any good father, disciplines us. When we wander away from him, God may bring us back through suffering. But this divine discipline is good because it teaches us to pay attention to God and his Word.

The Lord does many good things for us, such as teaching us and giving us good judgment and knowledge. This instruction from God, through the Bible and his Holy Spirit, is more valuable than millions in silver and gold and is available only to those who belong to Jesus.

PSALM 119 (YODH)

Verse 78: "Bring disgrace upon the arrogant people who lied about me; meanwhile, I will concentrate on your commandments."

Reflection:

When arrogant people smear God's children with lies—like they did to Jesus—God will bring disgrace upon them. But it is not up to us to concern ourselves with delivering justice. We are to concentrate on God and his Word and leave everything else to our heavenly Father.

God made us, he created us, and he will comfort us. He will surround us with his unfailing love and tender mercies as we delight in the Bible and follow his commands.

PSALM 119 (KAPH)

Verses 81-82: "I am worn out waiting for your rescue, but I have put my hope in your word. My eyes are straining to see your promises come true. When will you comfort me?"

Reflection:

Waiting is hard but waiting for God to answer a prayer that you really want is extremely difficult. Waiting requires patience, trust, strength, and endurance. But waiting time is not wasted time. God is working in the circumstances that you are praying about, and day by day, his plans are unfolding.

May you wait quietly and confidently for the Lord. And may you stay focused on him, putting your hope in the promises of his Word.

PSALM 119 (LAMEDH)

Verse 91: "Your regulations remain true to this day, for everything serves your plans."

Reflection:

God's Word is eternal—it remains forever. The Bible is as relevant today as the day it was written. God tells us in Scripture how he created the earth, how to have eternal life through faith in Jesus Christ, how time will end, and how eternity begins.

Everything that happens is serving God's plans and is moving us closer and closer to the second coming of Jesus. Believers can look forward with joy, even as wickedness continues to spread. God will sustain us with his faithfulness as we keep our mind on his instructions, but the wicked will die in misery.

PSALM 119 (MEM)

Verse 103-104: "How sweet your words taste to me; they are sweeter than honey. Your commandments give me understanding; no wonder I hate every false way of life."

Reflection:

Like the psalmist, may we:

➤ Read God's Word for guidance.
➤ Feast on the sweet words of Scripture to make us wiser than our enemies.
➤ Love the Lord's instructions and insight.
➤ Keep God's regulations, which give us wisdom.
➤ Think about the teaching of Jesus to keep us from turning away from him.
➤ Remain obedient to the Bible and walk on godly paths.

PSALM 119 (NUN)

Verse 105: "Your word is a lamp to guide my feet and a light for my path."

Reflection:

Six reasons to read the Bible are:

1. When you read the Bible every day, God uses it to guide you on the path of righteousness.
2. When you have a problem, God's Word has the answer.
3. When you learn to first turn to God in prayer and then turn to Scripture, he will give you the comfort and wisdom that you seek.
4. When you are determined to obey the Lord's instructions, his light and truth will guide you on the path of everlasting life.
5. When God's Word is your heart's delight, the wicked may set traps for you, but the Lord will watch over your path and protect you.
6. When you treasure the Bible and believe in Jesus, you won't have to walk in darkness because you will have the Light that leads to life.

PSALM 119 (SAMEKH)

Verse 114: "You are my refuge and my shield; your word is my source of hope."

Reflection:

For those who have received Jesus Christ as their Savior, our Father has given us the Holy Spirit to fill our hearts with his love and hope. Because God raised Jesus from the dead, we live with great expectations and look forward to the day when we, too, will live with our heavenly Father. And we will not be disappointed—our hope will be fulfilled.

Evil-minded people are only fooling themselves; God will skim them off the earth like scum. But Jesus, the Word who became flesh, is the hope of the world. He will sustain and rescue believers—our hope will not be crushed.

PSALM 119 (AYIN)

Verse 127: "Truly, I love your commands more than gold, even the finest gold."

Reflection:

What would you do if someone offered you gold in exchange for your Bible? For those who truly love God, giving away their Bible for a material possession is not even an option. You can't get truth from treasures. You can't get peace from pearls.

God speaks to his children through his Word, which is priceless. Our Father reminds us of his presence, power, promises, justice, and love. He teaches us about Jesus, the Holy Spirit, salvation, and the future. He shows us how to live and gives us hope. Nothing is more valuable than the Word of God—nothing.

PSALM 119 (PE)

Verse 136: "Rivers of tears gush from my eyes because people disobey your instructions."

Reflection:

This is how Jesus must feel about those who disobey the Bible, do not believe in him, and are destined for eternal death. If people would only listen to God, they would have light and life. If only they would accept his gift of salvation, God would ransom them from darkness and death.

The Lord looks upon the lost with love. He makes it so even simple-minded adults and children can understand the teaching of the Bible. May those who put their faith and trust in Jesus not be overcome by evil. May Jesus guide their steps by his Word. And may God show mercy to all who love Jesus and obey his instructions.

PSALM 119 (TSADHE)

Verse 143: "As pressure and stress bear down on me, I find joy in your commands."

Reflection:

Anxiety sprouts like a weed and strangles the truth of God's Word, choking out a life of peace. It causes us to focus on the wrong things. It diverts our attention away from the faithfulness of God and what he is doing in our lives today.

Turning to the Bible when we are feeling pressure and stress helps us to change our focus from our problems to God's promises. There is no better way to relieve stress than to listen to God speak through Scripture, which is perfectly true, thoroughly tested, completely trustworthy, and always right. The past is unchangeable, and the future is unknowable, but don't stress about it because God is in control of it all.

PSALM 119 (QOPH)

Verse 147: "I rise early, before the sun is up; I cry out for help and put my hope in your words."

Reflection:

Three key elements of starting your day with a balanced spiritual breakfast are:

1. Spending time with Jesus.

    Spending time with Jesus in his Word each morning is a good way to start your day with spiritual nourishment.

2. Meditating on the Bible.

    Meditating on the truth of the Bible gives you hope and reminds you of God's promises that will last forever.

3. Praying to the Lord.

    Praying to the Lord with all your heart—crying out to Jesus for help in prayer—helps you remember that he is near, gives you assurance that he hears your cry, and revives your soul because you know that, in his faithful love, God will answer.

PSALM 119 (RESH)

Verse 154: "Argue my case; take my side! Protect my life as you promised!"

Reflection:

The Holy Spirit convicts unbelievers of sin, so Satan, the Accuser, retaliates by accusing believers of wrongdoing. When this happens, the Lord Jesus Christ is our lawyer. Jesus argues our case before God the Father, reminding him that we are innocent because all our sins are covered by his blood.

As children of God, may we live honorable lives to silence the ignorant people who make foolish accusations against us. May we be like Jesus, who did not retaliate, but left his case in the hands of God. And may we remember and be encouraged by the promise that God will bless us with a great reward in heaven when people mock us, persecute us, lie about us, and say evil things against us because we are followers of Jesus.

PSALM 119
(SHIN)

Verse 162: "I rejoice in your word like one who discovers a great treasure."

Reflection:

Knowing Jesus and discovering God's Word is like finding a great treasure. The more time you spend reading the Bible, the more treasures you will find.

God gives us so many wonderful promises that it's hard not to get excited and praise him when you meditate on Scripture. And it's hard not to obey the Lord when you love him, love the Holy Bible, and are aware that he knows everything you do. Through his written Word, Jesus gives us light to see, prevents us from stumbling, and gives us great peace when we walk in obedience to him.

PSALM 119 (TAW)

Verse 176a: "I have wandered away like a lost sheep; come and find me..."

Reflection:

Before we know Jesus Christ as our Lord and Savior, we are lost, spiritually dead in sin, and destined for hell. But when we accept Jesus, we are found, forgiven, and born again spiritually. We are given eternal life and are headed for heaven.

Jesus said, "If a man has a hundred sheep and one of them gets lost, what will he do? Won't he leave the ninety-nine others in the wilderness and go to search for the one that is lost until he finds it? And when he has found it, he will joyfully carry it home on his shoulders. When he arrives, he will call together his friends and neighbors, saying, 'Rejoice with me because I have found my lost sheep.' In the same way, there is more joy in heaven over one lost sinner who repents and returns to God than over ninety-nine others who are righteous and haven't strayed away!" (Luke 15:4-7)

PSALM 120

Verse 2: "Rescue me, O Lord, from liars and from all deceitful people."

Reflection:

As long as we live on this earth, we will have to deal with lying and deceitful people. Jesus said that Satan, the father of lies, has always hated the truth because there is no truth in him. So when the devil, or those who belong to him, lie or do evil things, it is consistent with their character—dark.

Darkness and light have nothing in common. In fact, God separated them. "And God saw that the light was good. Then he separated the light from the darkness." (Genesis 1:4) May people of spiritual light—God's children through Christ—seek more light from Jesus and leave the deeds of darkness to those who will live in it forever.

PSALM 121

Verse 2: "My help comes from the Lord, who made heaven and earth."

Reflection:

The Lord Jesus himself watches over me. He never sleeps. He stands beside me day and night, protecting me from all harm. The Lord helps me, provides for me, protects me, and watches over my life—both now and forever.

Where does your help come from?

PSALM 122

Verse 6: "Pray for peace in Jerusalem. May all who love this city prosper."

Reflection:

Jerusalem is a holy city that is loved by God and his people. One day, all of God's children who bear his name will be citizens of the new Jerusalem that comes down from heaven. Zechariah prophesied to the people of Jerusalem that its righteous and victorious king would be coming, humbly riding on a donkey's colt. And we know that this is King Jesus, the Messiah (see John 12:14-16).

Jerusalem is the city where Jesus journeyed to, wept for, suffered and died in, and rose from the dead. As followers of Jesus and children of God, may we pray for peace in Jerusalem, the eternal city of God.

PSALM 123

Verse 1:   "I lift my eyes to you, O God, enthroned in heaven."

Reflection:

Where are your eyes looking—up to God or down at yourself? If you are focused on yourself, you will be fearful, worried, sad, and anxious because of your weakness and lack of control. But if you lift your eyes to God and look at him with eyes of faith, sitting on his glorious throne in heaven, you will be comforted by his power and holiness.

May you be encouraged when you look at God and remember his love, mercy, faithfulness, and presence. May you lift your eyes from yourself to God and trust his will, his perfect plan, and his control of everything. And may you be filled by the Holy Spirit with the joy and peace of Jesus.

PSALM 124

Verse 1a: "What if the Lord had not been on our side?"

Reflection:

I hate to think about what life would be like if the Lord were not on my side. I cannot imagine a future without the Lord on my side. And what about eternity without the Lord on my side—it is too frightening to contemplate.

The Lord Jesus is everything to me. He created me, loves me, and blesses me. He protects me, guides me, and gives me hope. Jesus is beside me, every moment of every day, leading me on the path that he has designed specifically for me. Jesus listens to my prayers—and answers—and comforts me with the peace of the Holy Spirit.

If the Lord were not on my side, I would be hopeless and overwhelmed with fear of the future. I would be nervous about the news and helplessly imprisoned by sin. But praise God! He saved my soul and is on my side forever!

PSALM 125

Verse 2:   "Just as the mountains surround Jerusalem, so the Lord surrounds his people, both now and forever."

Reflection:

Because the Lord surrounds his people,
   we are secure.

Because the Lord surrounds his people,
   we will not be defeated.

Because the Lord surrounds his people,
   we will endure forever.

Because the Lord surrounds his people,
   the wicked will not rule the land of the godly.

Because the Lord surrounds his people,
   he will banish those with crooked ways and take away those who do evil.

Because the Lord surrounds his people,
   he will do good to those whose hearts are in tune with his.

Because the Lord surrounds his people,
   we have peace.

PSALM 126

Verse 5: "Those who plant in tears will harvest with shouts of joy."

Reflection:

Planting is hard work. Sometimes it is so hard that it makes us cry and we want to give up. But God tells us in the Bible not to give up doing what is good, even if we have trouble.

If we trust in the Lord and rest in Jesus—who has overcome the world and all the trouble it contains—we can experience peace in him. And at just the right time, we will reap a harvest of blessings. We may weep as we go to plant the seed, but we will sing with joy about the amazing things the Lord has done when we return with the harvest!

PSALM 127

Verse 2: "It is useless for you to work so hard from early morning until late at night, anxiously working for food to eat; for God gives rest to his loved ones."

Reflection:

Unless the Lord is behind your work, it is a waste. But when your work is according to God's will, he will protect you and give you success.

Anxiously working from early morning until late at night is useless, according to God. Because we who belong to Jesus are children of God, he is the Source of our provision in every way. He is the farmer, he created the soil, he made the sun, and he provides the rain for food to grow. And God is the one who produces fruit in our lives.

So rather than being anxious, may we seek God first and rest in the truth that our Father will give us, his beloved, everything we need.

PSALM 128

Verse 1: "How joyful are those who fear the Lord—all who follow his ways!"

Reflection:

A Poem of Blessing

May the Lord bless you, who live in reverent fear of him.

May he bless you, who obey his Word, before your sight grows dim.

May the Lord grant you prosperity, fruitfulness, and joy.

May he bless you with a flourishing family and grandchildren to enjoy.

May the Lord continually bless you as you live and walk in his ways.

And may you experience his peace in all your days.

PSALM 129

Verse 5: "May all who hate Jerusalem be turned back in shameful defeat."

Reflection:

May those who hate Israel not receive the Lord's blessing.

May they be defeated, useless, ignored, and despised by God.

May God look down from his holy dwelling place in heaven and bless those who love Zion.

May God bless his people with mercy, peace, and freedom from persecution by their ungodly enemies.

And may the Lord of Heaven's Armies, the God of Israel, let Jerusalem endure forever.

PSALM 130

Verse 5: "I am counting on the Lord; yes, I am counting on him. I have put my hope in his word."

Reflection:

Call to the Lord. When you are in the depths of despair, call to the Lord for help. He will pay attention when you pray in Jesus' name and go to his throne in faith.

Count on the Lord. It is God's nature to keep his promises, and he delights when we come to him and ask him to do as he has promised in his Word.

Long for the Lord. Those who have accepted Jesus as their Savior long for his fellowship. When we spend time in the Bible and in an ongoing attitude of prayer, we become closer to Jesus and more aware of his presence.

Hope in the Lord. If it were not for the unfailing love of God, none of us could ever survive. But because his redemption overflows, our sins are forgiven and forgotten by our heavenly Father. We now have hope for today and for eternity.

PSALM 131

Verse 2b: "Yes, like a weaned child is my soul within me."

Reflection:

When a baby is weaned, it no longer cries for its mother's milk. Instead, the child learns to calm and quiet themselves. When we rest in God's all-sufficient love, we also learn to calm and quiet our hearts and to be content, letting our Father take care of us. We do not need to concern ourselves with matters too great for us to handle or understand. Instead, we can trust in the Lord to take care of us.

Jesus chose us, became a man for us, and died for us. He will surely take care of us—now and always.

PSALM 132

Verse 11:   "The Lord swore an oath to David with a promise he will never take back: 'I will place one of your descendants on your throne.'"

Reflection:

This is what the Lord said to David in reference to the coming Messiah, Jesus Christ, a descendant of David. Because King Jesus will sit on the throne in Jerusalem, the royal line of David will continue forever.

When Jesus returns to earth to reign, he will be a glorious king. When the new Jerusalem comes down from heaven, the Mighty One of Israel will be the light for his people. As God's faithful servants, we will be blessed and satisfied in our eternal home with Jesus, clothed with godliness and singing with joy!

PSALM 133

Verse 1: "How wonderful and pleasant it is when brothers live together in harmony."

Reflection:

Followers of Jesus, who are blessed with life everlasting, are to clothe themselves in love, which binds them together in perfect harmony. And when the body of Christ lives in harmony, peace, and unity, it is precious in our Father's eyes.

May we, brothers and sisters in Christ, be of one mind, united in thought and purpose. May we care for each other and build each other up. And may the God of love and peace be with you all.

PSALM 134

Verse 1a: "Oh, praise the Lord, all you servants of the Lord…"

Reflection:

Praise is a key element of the Christian life. When believers are filled with the Holy Spirit, they want to praise God. Singing songs to the Lord and making music with thankful hearts are two examples of praise.

Since we are receiving a kingdom that is unshakable, may we be thankful and please God by worshiping the Lord—who made heaven and earth—with holy fear and awe. May we offer, through Christ, a continual sacrifice of praise to God and proclaim our allegiance to his name. And may God, from his majestic throne above, shower us with his divine blessings and grace.

PSALM 135

Verse 5-6: "I know the greatness of the Lord—that our Lord is greater than any other god. The Lord does whatever pleases him throughout all heaven and earth, and on the seas and in their depths."

Reflection:

Unlike idols created by human hands, the uncreated Lord is the Creator of all things—including you.

➤ Idols have mouths but cannot speak, but the Lord is always speaking to you.

➤ Idols have eyes but cannot see, but the Lord sees everything you do.

➤ Idols have ears but cannot hear, but the Lord hears everything you think or say.

➤ Idols have mouths but cannot breathe, but the Lord is alive and gives you breath every day.

PSALM 136

Verse 1: "Give thanks to the Lord, for he is good! His faithful love endures forever."

Reflection:

Why should we give thanks to the Lord?

Because he is good, and his faithful love endures forever! He is the God of gods and the Lord of lords. He does mighty miracles. He made the heavens and placed the earth among the waters. He made the heavenly lights—the sun, moon, and stars. He remembers our weaknesses and saves us with a strong hand and powerful arm. He brings us out of our Egypt experience and leads us safely through the wilderness. He parts our Red Sea of impossibility and strikes down the enemy. He provides for every living thing. And he gives his people, his special possession, an eternal inheritance in heaven.

PSALM 137

Verse 4: "But how can we sing the songs of the Lord while in a pagan land?"

Reflection:

By not focusing on the pagan land, but instead focusing on our loving God and his goodness.

By remembering how God faithfully answered our prayers in the past and fights our battles today.

By forgiving, and watching God pay back our tormentors for what they have done to us.

By thanking God that not all the people in the pagan land are pagans.

By rejoicing in being chosen by God and rescued by the blood of Jesus Christ.

By making Jesus our greatest joy today and looking forward to being with him forever.

PSALM 138

Verse 8a: "The Lord will work out his plans for my life—for your faithful love, O Lord, endures forever."

Reflection:

The Lord God Almighty—the omnipotent, omniscient, and omnipresent Maker of heaven and earth—has plans for *my* life! His plan is a specific, moment by moment plan. And God's plan is good. It is wiser than the wisest of human plans.

God does not expect me to try to figure out his plan. The Lord will—not might, not maybe—work out his plans for me. He will determine the steps that I take. And he will make his plans succeed.

God saved me and called me to be righteous and holy in his eyes because that was his plan for me before the beginning of time—to show me his grace through Christ Jesus. And God, who began his good work in me, will continue his work until it is finally finished on the day when Jesus takes me home.

PSALM 139

Verse 17:   "How precious are your thoughts about me, O God. They cannot be numbered!"

Reflection:

God saw you before you were born. He laid out every moment of your life before a single day had passed.

God knit you together in your mother's womb. He watched you as you were being formed.

God knows everything about you. He knows the thoughts you think, your heart's desires, everything you do, and what you are going to say.

God goes before you and follows you. He places his hand of blessing on your head.

God is with you, day and night. He is guiding, supporting, and leading you along the path of everlasting life.

PSALM 140

Verse 13: "Surely, righteous people are praising your name; the godly will live in your presence."

Reflection:

The Lord will rescue those who belong to him from evil people and their evil schemes. He will protect the godly from violent people whose tongues sting like a snake and whose lips drip lies like venom from a viper.

Jesus will help the hopeless and rescue the righteous out of the hands of wicked people who stir up trouble and set traps. Our God will cause great disasters to fall on the proud who plot evil, and he will give justice to those that they persecute.

PSALM 141

Verse 4a: "Don't let me drift toward evil or take part in acts of wickedness."

Reflection:

Drifting sounds relaxing and peaceful—until you have drifted too far away, and you are in deep trouble. When we cut the ropes to fellowship with Jesus, we drift away from him.

May we listen carefully to what God says in his Word, believe it, and stand firmly in the truth. May we offer prayers as incense to the Lord each morning and evening. May we not partake in the delicacies of those who do wrong. And may our ropes of Bible study, prayer, and worship be securely attached to Jesus so we will not drift toward evil or take part in acts of wickedness.

PSALM 142

Verse 6a: "Hear my cry, for I am very low."

Reflection:

What should you do when you are feeling low and overwhelmed because it seems like no one cares?

- ➤ Cry out to the Lord—he will help you.
- ➤ Plead for the Lord's mercy—he is your place of refuge.
- ➤ Pour out your complaints to the Lord—he knows the way you should go.
- ➤ Tell all your troubles to the Lord—he will rescue you with his strength.
- ➤ Pray to the Lord—he loves you and cares about what happens to you.

Like the blind beggar (Luke 18:35-43), who would not stop shouting for Jesus to have mercy and give him sight, we should remember that persistence like his pays off. So keep calling on Jesus—in a whisper or a shout—because he hears you and he will show up at the right time. And when he does, remember to thank him for his help.

PSALM 143

Verse 10b: "May your gracious Spirit lead me forward on a firm footing."

Reflection:

When you read the Bible each morning, you will hear God speak to you.

When you give yourself to Jesus, he will show you where to walk.

When you trust in the Lord, you will experience his faithfulness.

When you run to the Good Shepherd to hide you, he will rescue you from your enemies.

When you are a child of God through Jesus, he will teach you to do his will.

When you are paralyzed with fear and losing hope, think about the great works of God and lift your heart to him in prayer.

When you are forced to live in darkness, Jesus will be your light and bring you out of your distress because of his unfailing love.

PSALM 144

Verse 15b: "Joyful indeed are those whose God is the Lord."

Reflection:

Joyful are those whose hands are trained and whose fingers are given skill by the Lord.

Joyful are those who call the Lord their ally, fortress, tower of safety, rescuer, shield, and refuge.

Joyful are those whose days are like a passing shadow, for they will spend eternity with the Lord.

Joyful are those who are given victory over their enemies by the Lord.

Joyful are those who flourish because the Lord is their provider.

Yes, joyful indeed are those who belong to the Lord Jesus Christ and live like this!

PSALM 145

Verses 1-2:   "I will exalt you, my God and King, and praise your name forever and ever. I will praise you every day; yes, I will praise you forever."

Reflection:

The Lord Jesus is good to everyone. He showers compassion on all his creation. The Lord Jesus always keeps his promises, and he is righteous in everything he does. The Lord Jesus does mighty acts, wonderful miracles, and awe-inspiring deeds. The Lord Jesus is filled with kindness. He helps the fallen and lifts those bent beneath their loads.

The Lord Jesus opens his hand and satisfies the hunger and thirst of every living thing. The Lord Jesus grants the desires of his faithful followers. He is close to all who call on him. The Lord Jesus protects those who love him, he hears their cries for help, and he rescues those who fear him. The Lord Jesus is slow to get angry and is filled with unfailing love—but he destroys the wicked.

PSALM 146

Verse 3: "Don't put your confidence in powerful people; there is no help for you there."

Reflection:

People, whether they are powerful or not, are just people—they are not God. When people breathe their last breath, they return to the earth. But God reigns forever! So put your hope and confidence in the Lord your God, and you will not be let down because he is faithful, and he loves the godly.

Those who have Jesus as their helper are lifted up and protected by the One who made heaven, earth, the sea, and everything in them. Those who belong to God, who keeps every promise forever, are also kept forever by his unfailing love.

The Lord protects and cares for his children. He gives justice to the oppressed and food to the hungry—but he frustrates the plans of the wicked. Therefore, "I will praise the Lord as long as I live. I will sing praises to my God with my dying breath." (verse 1b)

PSALM 147

Verse 5: "How great is our Lord! His power is absolute! His understanding is beyond comprehension!"

Reflection:

God the Father has life in himself, and he has granted that same life-giving power to Jesus Christ, God the Son. Jesus is now sitting at the place of power at the Father's right hand, and one day, when he returns, everyone will see Jesus coming on a cloud with power and great glory.

God heals the broken-hearted and counts the stars. He provides rain for the earth and feeds the wild animals. His thoughts are nothing like your thoughts, and his ways are far beyond anything you can imagine. It is impossible to understand the activity of God, who does all things. And since he is all-knowing and you are not, may you trust in the Lord with all your heart and not depend on your own understanding.

PSALM 148

Verse 5: "Let every created thing give praise to the Lord, for he issued his command, and they came into being."

Reflection:

What an amazing truth— "He issued his command, and they came into being." (verse 5b) God created everything through the Word, also known as Jesus Christ—nothing was created except through him. God the Father spoke the Word through God the Son and creation happened! Do you think that the Lord God cannot help you with the challenges in your life? He can!

"You are worthy, O Lord our God, to receive glory and honor and power. For you created all things, and they exist because you created what you pleased." (Revelation 4:11) Let every created thing praise the Lord!

PSALM 149

Verse 1a: "Sing to the Lord a new song."

Reflection:

Sing his praises. Tell everyone about God's wonderful deeds. Praise him for his holy splendor. Sing because the Lord, your Helper and Protector, is so good to you.

Sing for joy. Make music to the Lord in your heart and come before him singing with joy. Praise him while dancing. Shout joyfully to the Rock of our salvation.

Sing as you rest on your bed. Proclaim the Lord's unfailing love in the morning when you wake up and his faithfulness in the evening when you lay down. Praise God until your last breath.

Sing in the assembly of the faithful. Sing psalms, hymns, and spiritual songs to God with thankful hearts. Worship the Lord with gladness. May the people of God exult in their King and rejoice in their Maker.

PSALM 150

Verse 1a: "Praise the Lord!"

Reflection:

May our God be praised for his unequaled greatness and mighty works. May the Lord be continually praised in his sanctuary and in his mighty heaven.

May everything that breathes praise the Lord. May we praise him with the blast of a horn, a loud clash of symbols, tambourines, and dancing. May we praise him with a harp, flutes, and stringed instruments.

Whether loudly or softly, whether in stillness or with dancing, may everyone on earth praise God's holy name with all their heart and soul, forever and ever!

✧ ✧ ✧

The Book of
Proverbs

PROVERBS 1

Verse 7: "Fear of the Lord is the foundation of true knowledge, but fools despise wisdom and discipline."

Reflection:

Without Jesus as your Lord and Savior, you are a fool in God's eyes. Those who choose not to fear the Lord hate knowledge. People who pay no attention when the Holy Spirit reaches out and convicts them of their sin and their need for Christ lack discernment.

The Lord often calls to the unsaved, but they reject him and lack understanding. Simpletons lack insight and turn away from Jesus—to death. Fools despise wisdom and discipline and must eat the bitter fruit of living their own way: calamity, disaster, anguish, and distress. But all who belong to Jesus and listen to him will live in peace, untroubled by fear of harm.

PROVERBS 2

Verses 1-3: "My child, listen to what I say and treasure my commands. Tune your ears to wisdom and concentrate on understanding. Cry out for insight and ask for understanding."

Reflection:

The Lord grants wisdom to his children, who listen to what he says. From his Word comes knowledge and understanding. The Lord grants a treasure of common sense to the honest. He helps them recognize what is right, just, and fair. He shows them the right way to go.

Wisdom from God will save you from people who enjoy the twisted ways of evil and walk down dark paths that lead to death. Wise choices will watch over you. Understanding will keep you safe. And knowledge will fill you with joy. May the Lord shield those who walk with integrity, guard the paths of the just, and protect those who are faithful to him.

PROVERBS 3

Verse 1: "My child, never forget the things I have taught you. Store my commands in your heart."

Reflection:

Trust in the Lord with all your heart and seek his will in all you do, then he will show you which path to take.

Keep loyalty and kindness deep in your heart, then you will earn a good reputation and find favor with God and people.

Fear the Lord and turn away from evil, then you will have healing for your body and strength for your bones.

Honor the Lord with your wealth and the best part of everything you produce, then he will provide everything you need—and more!

Do not lose sight of common sense and discernment, then your feet will not stumble, and you will be safe on your way.

Remember that the Lord is your security, and he blesses the home of the upright, then you can go to bed without fear and sleep soundly.

PROVERBS 4

Verses 20-22: "My child, pay attention to what I say. Listen carefully to my words. Don't lose sight of them. Let them penetrate deep into your heart, for they bring life to those who find them, and healing to their whole body."

Reflection:

The instructions from our heavenly Father, found in the Bible, are the key to life. In him, we find wisdom and develop good judgment. When we listen and do as God says, we will have a long, good life—eternal life for those who believe in Jesus Christ.

May you always remain devoted to Jesus and cherish him above all else. May he give you wisdom to discern the right path and guide you along righteous ways. And may you diligently safeguard your heart and radiate the light of Christ in your inner being, shining ever brighter with each passing day.

PROVERBS 5

Verse 12:   "You will say, 'How I hated discipline! If only I had not ignored all the warnings!'"

Reflection:

We all have "if only" times in our past. Times when we wish we would have paid attention to people that God placed in our life and made better choices. Times when we wanted to do our own thing, our own way.

God warns us in the Bible to stay away from immoral people and to avoid having sex outside of marriage. He tells us of the consequences of sin and lack of self-control. Sin is like a rope that catches and holds us. It results in anguish, disease, and death. We cannot undo our sins and regrets of the past, but we can be forgiven for them by Jesus. Then, we can choose to walk forward on the path of life with our eyes on Jesus and our ears listening carefully to the wise counsel of his Word.

PROVERBS 6

Verse 16a: "There are six things the Lord hates—
no, seven things he detests:"

Reflection:

1. Haughty eyes – "Pride goes before destruction, and haughtiness before a fall." (Proverbs 16:18)

2. A lying tongue – Worthless and wicked people are constant liars.

3. Hands that kill the innocent – Cursed is anyone who accepts payment to kill an innocent person. The shedding of innocent blood, even the blood of the unborn, and the sacrifice of another person's life to the god of self is sinful.

4. A heart that plots evil – The perverted heart of the wicked plots evil, and they will be destroyed suddenly.

5. Feet that race to do wrong – Misery and destruction follows these people, and they do not know where to find peace. Among the living, they are like the dead.

6. A false witness who pours out lies – The Lord will repay his enemies for their evil deeds when

the courts oppose the righteous and justice is nowhere to be found.

7. A person who sows discord in a family – The wicked are constantly stirring up trouble, but they will be broken by God in an instant.

PROVERBS 7

Verse 2:   "Obey my commands and live! Guard my instructions as you guard your own eyes."

Reflection:

Your eyes are like a lamp that provides light for your whole body. So when they are healthy and looking at good things, your whole body is filled with light.

Before you accepted Jesus as your Savior, you were spiritually blind. However, after receiving him, your sins were forgiven, your eyes were opened, and your sight was restored, allowing you to see clearly.

May you diligently safeguard the Lord's instructions as you would your own eyes. Avoid letting your eyes wander and lead you into temptation. Instead, shift your focus from trivial matters and direct it towards the Word of God and the path of righteousness.

PROVERBS 8

Verses 1, 4-7: "Listen as Wisdom calls out! Hear as understanding raises her voice! 'I call to you, to all of you! I raise my voice for all people. You simple people, use good judgment. You foolish people, show some understanding. Listen to me! For I have important things to tell you. Everything I say is right, for I speak the truth and detest every kind of deception.'"

Reflection:

Wisdom is more valuable than rubies. Nothing you desire can compare to it. Common sense and success belong to wisdom. And all who love wisdom will surely find it.

Wisdom served as the architect when the Almighty created the world. Those who discover wisdom find life, joy, and receive favor. However, those who fail to find wisdom harm themselves. All who despise wisdom cherish death.

Where can you find wisdom? The Bible says, "For our benefit, God made him [Christ Jesus] to be wisdom itself." (1 Corinthians 1:30b)

PROVERBS 9

Verses 7-8: "Anyone who rebukes a mocker will get an insult in return. Anyone who corrects the wicked will get hurt. So don't bother correcting mockers; they will only hate you. But correct the wise, and they will love you."

Reflection:

Jesus is preparing a great banquet called the Wedding Feast of the Lamb. Everyone is invited and urged to come, but only those who accept the invitation— by putting their faith in Jesus—are blessed with life everlasting and wisdom.

The wise have good judgment and know to stay away from foolishness. They do not hate being corrected. They love to be instructed and become even wiser. The righteous love being taught and learning even more.

May wisdom that comes from the fear of the Lord multiply your days. May knowledge of the Holy One result in good judgment. And may godly correction and good teaching add years to your life.

PROVERBS 10

Verse 3: "The Lord will not let the godly go hungry, but he refuses to satisfy the craving of the wicked."

Reflection:

The godly are showered with blessings from the Lord, making them rich.

The earnings of the godly enhance their lives.

The words of the godly are a life-giving fountain, encouraging many.

The words of the godly are like sterling silver, helpful and full of wise advice.

The hopes of the godly will be granted and result in happiness.

When the storms of life come, the godly have a lasting foundation.

The godly will never be disturbed.

We have happy memories of the godly.

PROVERBS 11

Verse 19: "Godly people find life; evil people find death."

Reflection:

The wicked will fall under their load of sin.

When the wicked die, their aspirations cease to exist, as they had placed their trust in their own limited capabilities.

Godless people ruin their friendships with their mouths.

The whole city shouts for joy when the wicked perish.

Evil people get rich for the moment, but the reward of the godly will endure.

Evil people will certainly face punishment for their actions.

Because of God's divine justice, the godly can look forward to a reward, but the wicked can expect only judgment.

PROVERBS 12

Verse 25: "Worry weighs a person down; an encouraging word cheers a person up."

Reflection:

You might think that worry is somehow a virtue, but worry can actually be sinful because it is a failure to trust God. Nothing touches the Christian that has not first passed through the loving hands of God. Therefore, believers can rest in the Lord, knowing that he is in control and at work in their lives. No matter what your circumstances are, Jesus can—and will—carry you through them.

May you turn your worries into prayers. May you trust God. And may you let his peace guard your heart and mind.

PROVERBS 13

Verse 21: "Trouble chases sinners, while blessings reward the righteous."

Reflection:

God gives people a choice between blessings and curses. If they obey the Word of God, they will be showered with blessings. If they choose not to obey God, they will experience curses.

Those who accept Jesus as their Lord and Savior will experience blessings and have a right relationship with God. Those who reject Jesus and remain enemies of God will have trouble that goes from bad to worse.

Wickedness deprives people of wonderful blessings, and sin robs them of good things. But when Jesus hung on the cross, he took upon himself the curse for our wrongdoing. So those who put their faith in Christ become righteous and are rewarded with eternal life and blessings.

PROVERBS 14

Verse 34: "Godliness makes a nation great, but sin is a disgrace to any people."

Reflection:

When a nation rejects God and the Bible, it will decline. As God is removed from the fabric of a nation, so will he remove his blessings.

> ➤ When a country fails to see itself as "under God" but puts the will of wicked people above the will of holy God by passing laws to legalize sin, it will not prosper.
> ➤ How can a nation function "with liberty" when true liberty and freedom can only be found in Jesus Christ?
> ➤ God loves justice, and he has promised to deliver "justice for all."

But there is hope for wayward people and nations because the Bible says, "If we confess our sins to him, he is faithful and just to forgive us our sins and cleanse us from all wickedness." (1 John 1:9)

PROVERBS 15

Verse 28: "The heart of the godly thinks carefully before speaking; the mouth of the wicked overflows with evil words."

Reflection:

As followers of Christ, may we be careful not to sin in what we say. May we listen and hold our tongue unless we speak words of truth in kindness.

> ➤ The Lord delights in pure words. Do your words delight him?
> ➤ Everyone enjoys a fitting reply. Do you say the right thing at the right time?
> ➤ Gentle words are life giving and can deflect anger. Are your words gentle or harsh?
> ➤ The tongue of the wise makes knowledge appealing. Does your mouth speak words of wisdom from the Lord or belch out foolishness?

Little by little, may we become more like Jesus, serving the needs of others by listening with love. And when appropriate, may we have the wisdom to speak gentle words or, instead, choose to remain silent.

PROVERBS 16

Verse 9: "We can make our plans, but the Lord determines our steps."

Reflection:

God has carefully planned every moment of your life. Most people do not think about God or realize that he has sovereign control over every detail of their life. They think it's all up to them—they are in control, they make their plans, and they make them happen. But that is not true. So it is wise to pray and commit our actions to the Lord, relying on him to make our plans succeed. When we talk to our Father about our plans and his will for our life, he will give us the right answer, and we will see that his way is always best.

Before we knew Jesus as our Lord and Savior, we were following a path that seemed right to us, but that path led to disappointment, destruction, and would have ended in death. But thank God, Jesus led us away from evil and put us on a path that leads to abundant and eternal life in him!

PROVERBS 17

Verse 22a: "A cheerful heart is good medicine."

Reflection:

When doubt and worry fill your mind, God's Word will comfort you and give you renewed hope and cheer. That is why it is very important to read the Bible. There may be a promise in the Scriptures that fits your situation, but if you are not aware of it, you will miss its comfort. You are like a prisoner holding a ring full of keys. There may be one key that will unlock the door and set you free, but if you do not look for it, you will remain a prisoner.

You should be familiar with what God says in his Book, then you can turn to his promises and be revived and comforted whenever you face difficulty and doubt. And that is good medicine!

PROVERBS 18

Verse 21: "The tongue can bring death or life; those who love to talk will reap the consequences."

Reflection:

A person has truly great power if they have power over themselves, including power over their tongue. Listening more than talking takes self-discipline but spouting off before listening is both shameful and foolish.

Biblical love is selfless and so is letting others speak while you listen—without inserting yourself. But unfriendly people care only about themselves and lash out at common sense. They are weak and lack self-control. Fools have no interest in understanding or listening to others. They only want to air their own opinions, which often leads to quarrels. Eventually, the mouth of fools will be their ruin when they trap themselves with their lips.

PROVERBS 19

Verse 3: "People ruin their lives by their own foolishness and then are angry at the Lord."

Reflection:

There are countless ways that people ruin their lives: laziness, immorality, talking too much, losing their temper, being undisciplined, lying, and drunkenness to name a few. But it all boils down to sin and disobedience to God.

Fear of the Lord leads to life, bringing security and protection from harm. By keeping God's commandments, you will keep your life but despising them will lead to death. Jesus said, "But even more blessed are all who hear the word of God and put it into practice." (Luke 11:28)

PROVERBS 20

Verse 24: "The Lord directs our steps, so why try to understand everything along the way?"

Reflection:

Jesus said, "A branch cannot bear fruit if it is severed from the vine, and you cannot be fruitful unless you remain in me." (John 15:4b) The primary duty of the branch is to cling to the vine. Christians tend to miss this. Our goal is not to bear fruit, our goal is to stay attached.

When a parent guides a child through a bustling street, they gently grasp the child's hand and give them a simple, yet crucial, responsibility: "Hold my hand." Similarly, God extends his hand to us, inviting us to place our trust in him. Our primary goal is not to understand every detail along the path or have complete knowledge of the future. Rather, our focus should be on firmly holding the hand of the One who possesses infinite wisdom—and never, ever letting go.

PROVERBS 21

Verse 1: "The king's heart is like a stream of water directed by the Lord; he guides it wherever he pleases."

Reflection:

As the days draw nearer to the anticipated return of Christ, it is expected that there will be an increase in wars and threats of wars as foretold by Jesus in the twenty-fourth chapter of the New Testament book of Matthew.

It is important for believers to remember that God is in sovereign control over all things, including the actions of world leaders. While we may not always agree with their decisions, we must trust that God's plan is unfolding just as he revealed in the Bible. As we pray for the salvation of others in these times of global unrest and conflict, let us draw strength and courage from the knowledge that our security lies in Christ, not in human leaders. Ultimately, the victory belongs to the Lord!

PROVERBS 22

Verse 19: "I am teaching you today—yes, you—
so you will trust in the Lord."

Reflection:

The Bible is God's book, his holy Word, that he has given to us. God speaks to us through his Word like a divine text message and teaches us about himself and how we are to live as his children. God tells us that he will direct us on the right path, which leads to riches, honor, and long life. Our Father warns us of the consequences for being corrupt and disobedient. He advises us not to be lazy, immoral, or hot tempered. Rather, as followers of Jesus, we should be pure, honest, gracious, humble, and generous.

Before reading Scripture, may we pray and ask the Lord to open our eyes to see and our mind to understand the truth that he reveals. And after meditating on his Word, may we pray and ask the Holy Spirit to help us in applying our hearts to his teachings.

PROVERBS 23

Verse 29: "Who has anguish? Who has sorrow? Who is always fighting? Who is always complaining? Who has unnecessary bruises? Who has bloodshot eyes?"

Reflection:

Who has anguish?

➢ People who put their trust and security in money rather than in Jesus—they wear themselves out trying to get rich.

➢ People who are stingy and always thinking about how much it costs.

Who has sorrow?

➢ Fools who despise wise, godly advice and do not listen to knowledge or seek instruction.

Who is always fighting?

➢ People who cheat others and take advantage of the defenseless. God, our Redeemer, will personally give them justice.

Who is always complaining?

> Those who envy sinners and do not fear the Lord. They fail to keep their heart on the right course and do not say what is right.

Who has unnecessary bruises?

> People who carouse with drunkards and feast with gluttons.
> Those who delight in prostitutes rather than in following God's ways.

Who has bloodshot eyes?

> Those who spend long hours drinking. Don't even look at it or you will be tempted. In the end, it will bite you like a poisonous snake. It will sting you like a viper and leave you unsatisfied

PROVERBS 24

Verse 23a: "Here are some further sayings of the wise:"

Reflection:

"Don't envy people or desire their company. For their hearts plot violence and their words always stir up trouble." (verses 1-2)

"Don't go to war without wise guidance; victory depends on having many advisers." (verse 6)

"Don't excuse yourself by saying, 'Look, we didn't know.' For God understands all hearts, and he sees you. He who guards your soul knows you knew. He will repay all people as their actions deserve." (verse 12)

"Don't rejoice when your enemies fall; don't be happy when they stumble. For the Lord will be displeased with you and will turn his anger away from them." (verses 17-18)

"Don't fret because of evildoers; don't envy the wicked. For evil people have no future; the light of the wicked will be snuffed out." (verses 19-20)

"Don't associate with rebels for disaster will hit them suddenly." (verses 21b-22a)

PROVERBS 25

Verse 2:   "It is God's privilege to conceal things and the king's privilege to discover them."

Reflection:

Reading God's Word is like searching for hidden treasure. The Bible is full of valuable gems of truth for us to discover. God's riches, wisdom, and knowledge are immeasurable! God's gifts found in Scripture are inexhaustible! As the Lord reveals things to you in the Bible, you will treasure his Word—it will become your heart's delight. But even better, the Almighty Author himself will be your most precious treasure.

Jesus said, "Wherever your treasure is, there the desires of your heart will also be." (Luke 12:34) He also said, "Yes, a person is a fool to store up earthly wealth but not have a rich relationship with God." (Luke 12:21) Have you discovered a rich relationship with Jesus? Keep searching God's treasure map until you find it.

PROVERBS 26

Verse 1: "Honor is no more associated with fools than snow with summer or rain with harvest."

Reflection:

The True Nature of Fools

➤ Fools are not trustworthy.
➤ Fools are not good employees.
➤ Fools are lazy.
➤ Fools cannot control their mouth.
➤ Fools argue, gossip, and deceive.
➤ Fools set traps for others and get caught in it themselves.
➤ Fools have hearts full of evil.
➤ Fools repeat their foolishness.
➤ Fools think they are wise.
➤ Fools have no hope.
➤ Fools do not know how to interpret the present times.
➤ Fools refuse to accept the truth that would save them.
➤ Fools do not have a relationship with God through Jesus Christ.

PROVERBS 27

Verse 1:   "Don't brag about tomorrow, since you don't know what the day will bring."

Reflection:

The Bible tells us that it is evil to boast about our own pretentious plans (see James 4:16). Our confidence should not be in ourselves, but in God. And since we do not know what God has planned for us from one moment to the next, how do we know what our life will look like tomorrow? The truth is that we do not know, and we may not even be here when tomorrow comes.

Rather than dwelling on what we plan to do tomorrow, may we adopt the mindset of surrendering to the Lord's will and following his guidance moment by moment. Instead of prioritizing fleeting pleasures, such as an upcoming vacation, may we focus on nurturing our relationship with Christ and preparing for our eternal destination.

PROVERBS 28

Verse 13: "People who conceal their sins will not prosper, but if they confess and turn from them, they will receive mercy."

Reflection:

There is a similar passage in the New Testament: "If we claim we have no sin, we are only fooling ourselves and not living in the truth. But if we confess our sins to him, he is faithful and just to forgive us our sins and to cleanse us from all wickedness." (1 John 1:8-9)

Confession of your sins to God and accepting Jesus—the sacrifice that atones for your sins and the sins of all the world—as your Savior is how all your sins are forgiven. It is also how you are reborn spiritually into the family of God and blessed with eternal life. In addition, when you accept God's gift of salvation, you receive the Holy Spirit who lives within you, teaches you, and empowers you to live the Christian life.

PROVERBS 29

Verse 6: "Evil people are trapped by sin, but the righteous escape, shouting for joy."

Reflection:

Sin is the devil's trap, and it is easy to fall into. Deception is one of the tricks that he uses to lure people into the trap of sin. Once a person is trapped, they are held captive by Satan to do whatever he wants. If they do not escape, they are doomed to destruction. But there is a way to escape the trap of sin—by accepting Jesus Christ as your Savior and Lord.

For those who belong to Christ, the power of the life-giving Holy Spirit frees them from the power and slavery of sin that leads to death. You can try to free yourself from sin and you may succeed temporarily, but if Jesus sets you free, you are truly free. Sin is a spiritual battle, and those who are made righteous by the blood of Jesus will shout for joy as they live victoriously in freedom!

PROVERBS 30

Verse 5a: "Every word of God proves true."

Reflection:

The Bible is the Word of God. It is inspired by God, and it is trustworthy and true—every word, every promise.

True—Jesus is the truth.

> ➤ Jesus said, "I am the way, the truth, and the life. No one can come to the Father except through me." (John 14:6)

True—Jesus is the Son of God.

> ➤ "And we know that the Son of God has come, and he has given us understanding so that we can know the true God. And now we live in fellowship with the true God because we live in fellowship with his Son, Jesus Christ. He is the only true God, and he is eternal life." (1 John 5:20)

True—To deny Jesus is to deny God.

> ➤ "Anyone who denies the Son doesn't have the Father, either. But anyone who acknowledges the Son has the Father also." (1 John 2:23)

True—Eternal life comes through faith in Jesus.

➤ "Jesus told her, 'I am the resurrection and the life. Anyone who believes in me will live, even after dying.'" (John 11:25)

True—Jesus is coming again.

➤ "Look, I am coming soon! Blessed are those who obey the words of prophecy written in this book." (Revelation 22:7)

PROVERBS 31

Verse 30: "Charm is deceptive, and beauty does not last; but a woman who fears the Lord will be greatly praised."

Reflection:

May followers of Jesus make themselves attractive by the good things they do, which comes from a heart of love. May godly people who are kind, helpful, trustworthy, strong, and hardworking be rewarded. May believers who are wise and do not suffer from laziness be blessed. And may Christians who speak up for the helpless and have no fear, except for their fear of the Lord, be praised.

✧ ✧ ✧

The Book of
Ecclesiastes

ECCLESIASTES 1

Verse 9: "History merely repeats itself. It has all been done before. Nothing under the sun is truly new."

Reflection:

Like the sun rises and sets every day, history repeats itself. There is a cycle of life—birth, growth, and death. There is a cycle of sin—sin, repentance, forgiveness. Remember the days of Noah when everyone except Noah and his family was completely sinful, and God destroyed every living thing with water. So it will be in the end. The people of the world will become more and more sinful, and God will destroy every living thing, except those who belong to Jesus, with fire. History repeats itself.

You would think that people would learn from the past, but we don't remember what happened in the past, so God has given us the Bible. Scripture refreshes our memory of the past, warns us about the future, and reminds us how to live in the present. Chasing after the things of the world is meaningless, but chasing after Jesus and the things of heaven gives true satisfaction and contentment.

ECCLESIASTES 2

Verse 2,3b,8b: "I said to myself, 'Come on, let's try pleasure. Let's look for the "good things" in life.'"

"I tried to experience the only happiness most people find during their brief life in this world."

"I had everything a man could desire."

Reflection:

Whether you put your energy into pleasure, work, wisdom, or wealth—it is all meaningless without God. Because everything good comes from the hand of God, you cannot truly enjoy what he gives you apart from a relationship with him through Jesus.

Everything you work so hard to accomplish is meaningless without God. All the things you acquire will not give you happiness without God. There is no value in wisdom without God.

To have all the "good things" of the world but not have Jesus is a miserable existence. But belonging to Jesus Christ, living in his love, and having complete assurance of your union with him is the ultimate fulfillment.

ECCLESIASTES 3

Verse 11a: "Yet God has made everything beautiful for its own time. He has planted eternity in the human heart…"

Reflection:

Like delicate flowers of the field, we cannot expect to bloom forever. During periods of frailty and illness, may we, as followers of Jesus, honor God even in our suffering. Soon we will be transplanted into the garden of heaven, so let's not sink our roots too deeply into the soil of earth.

May we not set our affections on the things of earth because the hour that they must be returned to the Lender could be very near. For everything there is a season—a time to be born, a time to bloom, and a time to die—so let's set our sights on eternity and the realities of heaven.

ECCLESIASTES 4

Verse 9: "Two people are better off than one, for they can help each other succeed."

Reflection:

God works through the people that he places in our lives—

- ➢ People who express love through words, prayers, and listening.
- ➢ People who provide comfort and encouragement.
- ➢ People who understand the painful circumstances we endure because they have been through it.
- ➢ People who can reach out and help us if we fall.

Jesus cares for us and loves us by sending people to help us conquer the difficulties of life.

ECCLESIASTES 5

Verse 10b: "How meaningless to think that wealth brings true happiness!"

Reflection:

God says that those who love money will never have enough, but those who love God receive wealth and good heath to enjoy it as a gift from him. The rich seldom get a good night's sleep. They hoard their riches and harm themselves by worrying about losing everything. But God gives rest to his loved ones—without fear, they lie down and sleep soundly.

We all come to the end of our lives as naked and empty-handed as on the day we were born. We can't take our riches with us, so what good is wealth except to watch it slip through your fingers? But our riches that are stored in heaven, because we belong to Jesus, are safe.

So if you are rich in this world, don't be proud and don't put your trust in money, which is so unreliable. Your trust should be in God, who is always reliable. He will never fail you and he will give you all that you need to keep you busy enjoying life!

ECCLESIASTES 6

Verse 9a: "Enjoy what you have rather than desiring what you don't have."

Reflection:

What is the point of living to an old age if you don't have satisfaction in life? If you spend your life working just so you can live, but you never seem to have enough— what is the answer to this type of existence?

As a child of God, we find our contentment in Jesus. He is our everything—our Savior, our Lord, our Provider. Being thankful for what he gives us, where he leads us, and his plans for our lives results in joy and contentment. And "true godliness with contentment is itself great wealth." (1 Timothy 6:6) So enjoy what you have and trust Jesus with every aspect of your life.

Everything has been decided. It was known long ago what each person would be, so do not argue with God about your destiny. Instead, align your will with God's perfect will, and then you will live each day with true joy and contentment.

ECCLESIASTES 7

Verse 4: "A wise person thinks a lot about death, while a fool thinks only about having a good time."

Reflection:

There is not a single person on earth who always does good and never sins. And nothing is certain in this life except that everyone dies. So the living should take this to heart before it is too late.

Only wisdom that comes from God can save your life and only by faith in Jesus Christ can you have eternal life. With Jesus as your Savior, a house in heaven, and an eternal body to look forward to, you can truly know that "the day you die is better than the day you are born." (verse 1b)

ECCLESIASTES 8

Verse 14b: "In this life, good people are often treated as though they were wicked, and wicked people are often treated as though they were good. This is so meaningless!"

Reflection:

In this life, people have the power to hurt each other, and wicked criminals are sometimes buried with honor. But those who are wise will find a time and a way to do what is right. For even though a person sins a hundred times and still lives a long life, those who fear God will be better off by far.

People cannot avoid what they do not know will happen. None of us can prevent or escape the day that God has chosen for our death, and we cannot hold back our spirit from departing our body. Therefore, it is important to always be ready to die and to know where you will spend eternity. Because in the face of death, wickedness will certainly not rescue the wicked from hell, but God will welcome into heaven those who have received the Lord Jesus by faith.

ECCLESIASTES 9

Verse 12: "People can never predict when hard times might come. Like fish in a net or birds in a trap, people are caught by sudden tragedy."

Reflection:

Everyone will experience troubles and sorrows as they live in this world. Jesus said, "But take heart, because I have overcome the world." (John 16:33b) When tragedy strikes, with Jesus by our side, we can be overcomers too.

People who are corrupted by evil have no hope, no rewards, and nothing ahead of them but death and hell. But believers have hope in Jesus and eternal life in heaven to look forward to. May we rejoice in our confident hope, be patient in trouble, and keep on praying. And may we remember that nothing—not even trouble or tragedy—can ever separate us from the love of Christ.

ECCLESIASTES 10

Verse 7: "I have seen servants riding horseback like princes—and princes walking like servants!"

Reflection:

When Jesus—the King of kings—came down from heaven to earth, he lived as a servant and died as a criminal. So it makes sense that followers of Christ are looked down on by the world.

Even in the workplace, Christians who have proven their worth may be given a low position or even lose their job for their beliefs, while great authority is given to fools. As believers, we should reflect Jesus in our jobs, have a quiet spirit, and not quit if our boss is angry with us. The wicked may be riding high now, but when Jesus returns, the lowest will rise and the highest will fall. What happens in the world is often upside down, but eternity will right the wrongs of time.

"Then he [Jesus] said, 'I tell you the truth, unless you turn from your sins and become like little children, you will never get into the Kingdom of Heaven. So anyone who becomes as humble as this little child is the greatest in the Kingdom of Heaven.'" (Matthew 18:3-4)

ECCLESIASTES 11

Verse 5:

"Just as you cannot understand the path of the wind or the mystery of a tiny baby growing in its mother's womb, so you cannot understand the activity of God, who does all things."

Reflection:

We cannot know what lies ahead, but we can know that there will be some dark days. And when they come, if our relationship with Jesus is strong, we will stand firm.

We cannot always understand the activity of God, but we can be assured that he is a good Father, a loving Savior, and a trustworthy Helper. So rather than trying to figure out God's next move, as his child, may we trust him, refuse to worry, and rejoice in every new day of life.

ECCLESIASTES 12

Verse 1: "Don't let the excitement of youth cause you to forget your Creator. Honor him in your youth before you grow old and say, 'Life is not pleasant anymore.'"

Reflection:

Listen carefully to God, study his Word, and obey his commands. They may be painful at times, but they are helpful.

Fear God, for he will judge us for everything we do—including every secret thing—whether good or bad.

Honor God with your life, your work, and your body while you are able. Don't wait until you grow old, your sight grows dim, your hearing grows faint, and your strength grows weak.

Remember God before you near the grave. Life is short, and before you know it, your body will return to the dust of the earth and your spirit will return to God who gave it.

✧ ✦ ✧

The Book of
Song of Songs

SONG OF SONGS 1

Verse 2: "Kiss me and kiss me again, for your love is sweeter than wine."

Reflection:

The love of Christ for his bride, the church, is better than any love we can ever imagine. It is a sacred, selfless, and sinless love—a perfect love.

When Jesus turned water into wine at the wedding in Cana, the master of ceremonies (not knowing where it had come from) declared, "A host always serves the best wine first. Then, when everyone has had a lot to drink, he brings out the less expensive wine. But you have kept the best until now!" (John 2:10)

Similarly, Christ's love for us is the best. No worldly delights can compare with one sip of the love of Jesus— the only true delight. And no wine can rival the love of Christ for his beloved bride.

SONG OF SONGS 2

Verse 15: "Catch all the foxes, those little foxes, before they ruin the vineyard of love, for the grapevines are blossoming!"

Reflection:

Sin, even "little sins", can be compared to little foxes. If they are not caught, they can ruin a person.

People, especially Christians, should be careful not to think lightly of "little sins". They can damage the connection between the branch and the Vine and prevent the blossoms from producing fruit. If not caught like a fox, "little sins" become familiar, unnoticed, and acceptable as they continue to slowly poison the branch and spoil the grapes that might have been produced for the Kingdom of God.

"Little sins" are what sent Jesus to the cross and caused him to suffer and die—that is how big "little sins" really are!

SONG OF SONGS 3

Verse 6:   "Who is this sweeping in from the wilderness like a cloud of smoke? Who is it, fragrant with myrrh and frankincense and every kind of spice?"

Reflection:

Like the young woman who yearned for and sought her husband, may we yearn for and seek Jesus Christ. And once we have found him and accepted him as our Savior and Lord, may we hold him tightly, so we do not lose our close fellowship with him.

Jesus is the Messiah, who will one day return, sweeping in like a cloud of smoke. Jesus is our High Priest, fragrant with frankincense. Jesus is the Lamb of God, who was sacrificed for us, and whose body was wrapped in myrrh and spices. But Jesus is also our King and Bridegroom, who is looking forward to his most joyous day—his wedding day!

SONG OF SONGS 4

Verse 7: "You are altogether beautiful, my darling, beautiful in every way."

Reflection:

Jesus loves everything about his bride. He is not only delighted at her external beauty but also at her internal beauty and love. Jesus himself is the reason that his bride is entirely beautiful and without blemish or stain of sin—he made her that way with his precious blood.

God said, "It is not good for the man to be alone. I will make a helper who is just right for him." (Genesis 2:18) Similarly, the Father is making the true church to be a bride that is "just right" for his Son, Jesus.

Before Adam and Eve sinned, they lived in a perfect paradise and had communion with God in the Garden of Eden. When we are united with Jesus as his bride, we will, in a sense, go back to the garden and live with him in our heavenly home that is illuminated by the glory of God...forever and ever!

SONG OF SONGS 5

Verse 1b: "Oh, lover and beloved, eat and drink!
Yes, drink deeply of your love!"

Reflection:

Jesus is better than countless others. He loves you and wants to be your best friend and the love of your life.

Jesus said, "Anyone who is thirsty may come to me! Anyone who believes in me may come and drink!" (John 7:37b-38a) Are you spiritually thirsty? Believe in Jesus and drink of his salvation. You can't earn it or pay for it—it's free! Then you will have rivers of living water, the Holy Spirit, flowing from the lover of your soul to you, his beloved.

"I slept, but my heart was awake when I heard my lover knocking and calling…" (verse 2a) When you hear Jesus knocking on the door of your heart and calling to you to open the door, don't wait. Jump out of bed, run to the door, unlock it, and open it! Because if you hesitate and open the door when it's more convenient for you, Jesus might be gone.

SONG OF SONGS 6

Verse 1: "Where has your lover gone, O woman of rare beauty? Which way did he turn so we can help you find him?"

Reflection:

What a relief to know that God is omnipresent! He is always with us, no matter where we are. And as children of God, indwelled by the Holy Spirit, we will never have to ask where Jesus has gone. Even though it may sometimes feel as though Jesus is gone, in reality, he is not. It is our indifference that prevents us from experiencing his presence. The more we abide in Jesus, the more we become like him, and the deeper our fellowship with him will be.

Jesus said, "And be sure of this: I am with you *always,* even to the end of the age." (Matthew 28:20b) His presence can be experienced. His promise is as true today as the day he said it. Jesus delights to be with us, and he will be found by those who seek him wholeheartedly.

SONG OF SONGS 7

Verse 10: "I am my lover's, and he claims me a his own."

Reflection:

God knew us before he formed us in our mothers' wombs. Even before he made the world, God loved us and chose to adopt us into his family through Jesus Christ—making us holy and without fault in his eyes, which is how the young man feels about his wife.

God sets us apart and claims us as his children, brothers and sisters of Christ, who progressively resemble Jesus in our character, conduct, and conversation. God chose us in advance and called us to come to him. He claims us as his own and has given us an inheritance. He has given us right standing with himself and he has given us his glory!

May we, who are claimed by God as his own, be pleasing to him in every way as we give Jesus the best of our love!

SONG OF SONGS 8

Verse 6b: "Love flashes like fire, the brightest kind of flame."

Reflection:

The love of God for his children is fierce. On earth, we are permanently sealed as belonging to God by the Holy Spirit when we receive Jesus Christ as our Savior. In heaven, we will have his name written on our foreheads.

God's love for his children is strong, jealous, and enduring. He tells us, "You must worship no other gods, for the Lord, whose very name is Jealous, is a God who is jealous about his relationship with you." (Exodus 34:14) And because God is a jealous God, he is a devouring fire. His love is unequaled, flaming like a furnace within the hearts of his children.

God is always thinking of us; his heart continually yearns for us, and he is always working things out for our good. Jesus has set us like a seal on his arm. His love is as strong as death. And just as God raised Christ Jesus from the dead, we are raised from death to life by the same Spirit living in us.

The love of God for his children cannot be quenched or drowned. It is not something that can be bought with all the wealth in the world. Rather, God's love is a priceless gift that is given to us freely.

Printed in the United States
by Baker & Taylor Publisher Services